© Copyright 1994 by Randy Barber

Cover design by Graphic Press, Inc.

Edited by Jean Candler

Typeset in 11 pt. Times
by Graphic Services, Inc., Tacoma, WA.

Library of Congress Catalog Number: 85-63794

ISBN 0-937125-05-9

Printed in USA

DECISION BOOKS

PREFACE

Beyond the compulsion I feel to fulfill my calling to the ministry, I have but one goal in mind as I write. That goal is to explain the Word of God in a manner that will be more readable than the typical scholarly work, yet at a depth that will challenge the thinking, gain the interest, and earn the respect of the more inquiring mind. I pray that I have met that goal in this book.

Scripture quotations in this book are from the *Authorized King James Version* of the Bible. Out of respect for God, I have taken the liberty to capitalize any reference made to Him while quoting from Scripture. I have also capitalized the *Sabbath* of the Moral Law so as to more easily distinguish it from the *sabbaths* of the Ceremonial Law.

I only ask that you read this book with a prayful attitude, and humbly consider its content. My desire is that this book become a catalyst to launch you into a deeper relationship with God and His Word.

INDEX

GOD ASKED US TO REMEMBER

We all have special moments in time when we stop our hustle and bustle long enough to remember. There is the special moment of a Centennial celebration when we remember the history of our country. There is the special moment of the Fourth of July when we remember our struggle for independence. There is the special moment of New Year's Eve when we remember the past year. There is the special moment of a family reunion when we remember our roots. There is also the special moment of a birthday.

Every time my children have a birthday, I cannot help but look back with fondness and retrace their growth right back to that special day when they came into this world. I get a warm glow inside as I remember the bond of love that has always existed between us. Because I love my children, their birthdays have always been very special to me.

Our Heavenly Father loves His children as well, and He too longs for those "birthdays." He longs for those special times together, remembering. But it was not enough for God that we stop and remember only once a year. He knew that it would be too easy for us to forget our roots if too much time elapsed, so when He made this world, He arranged for us all to have a special "birthday party" once a week. Yes, once a week! After all, who said that birthdays should be celebrated only once a year?

At the end of creation week God set aside a special day of rest (Genesis 2:1-3) as a memorial of creation. It was to be a special time for man to look back and remember. When we celebrate this special creation rest, we are celebrating the "birthday" of this world. We are celebrating God's power to create. We are remembering our Heavenly Father. We are remembering our family roots. We are remembering where we came from and where we are going.

The most precious gift that God has given to us (outside of salvation) is this special weekly time to rest and remember. If we observe it as He intended, it will protect us against the disease of materialism and status-seeking, for it is a day in which both "worldly pleasure" and "business" become unimportant. If we observe it as He intended, it will protect us against idolatry and selfishness, for it is a day when we are to look away from ourselves and look to Him.

If the human family had observed God's special rest day from creation as He intended, there would never have been any such thing as idol worship, for we would have celebrated God's creative power each week. We would have celebrated the "birthday" of this world each week. We would have celebrated our roots each week. And all this celebrating would have kept things so fresh in our minds that we would not have had time to forget.

I was born on March 27 and my older brother was born on April 6. Because our birthdays were only ten days apart, our parents would often celebrate them together around the first of April (it was their way of playing an April Fools' joke). I remember a number of times when we both invited all of our classmates to one of these joint celebrations on our farm in Colorado. And I can still remember thinking that this was a great deal for Gary because he received his gifts several days early. I, on the other hand, always felt cheated because I had to wait for several days after my birthday to get mine.

I still remember everyone filing by as the party ended, wishing us "Happy Birthday" one last time. Something didn't feel quite right about it, though. That day was not

6

my birthday! It always felt anticlimactic. The thrill of my birthday had worn off several days before the party began.

As we grew older and the practice of celebrating joint birthdays ended, that "after the fact" feeling ended as well. I remember distinctly that it felt good to celebrate my birthday on the actual anniversary of the date of my birth, and not on some other unrelated day.

WHICH DAY IS IT?

As I sat in my office one morning reading my mail, the phone rang. The lady on the other end asked if I would please come over to her house right away. Wondering what might be the problem, I quickly drove to the address she gave me. As I took a seat in her living room she said, "I think that I have been going to church all these years on the wrong day. Could you please help me?"

That visit took place many years ago, and since then I have received dozens of inquiries like it. It is questions like these that have prompted me to write what you are about to read.

It is very clear from reading the Bible that the Lord set aside one day out of seven as a day of rest; a day when we are to put aside our earthly cares and rest from our labors. The Islamic faith believes that special day to be Friday. Sabbatarians believe it to be Saturday, while the rest of Christianity, in general, believes it to be Sunday. **Which day is it**? **Does it really matter**? **Can it be all three**? **Does my salvation depend on it**? These are only a few of the questions that I am asked as I visit with people day after day. Let's see if we can find the answers.

To begin with, I must state that I believe the Bible is God's inspired Word. 2 Timothy 3:16,17 says: *"All scripture is given by inspiration of God, and is profitable for doctrine, for reproof, for correction, for instruction in righteousness: That the man of God may be perfect, throughly furnished unto all good works."* The Bible is God's revelation to me. It is my "roadmap" to heaven. To

7

keep from getting lost, I must study it carefully and then be willing to follow what it tells me to do. I also realize that I must not base my belief on only one or two isolated texts, but must study it *"here a little, and there a little"* (Isaiah 28:10) so as to get a more complete understanding of what the Lord is trying to say to me. With this in mind, let us proceed.

Many people today believe that one day is just like any other day. But it is clear from plain Scriptural statements that our Lord recognizes one specific day as His day. In Revelation 1:10 John said: *"I was in the Spirit on the Lord's day."* We can see from this text that the Lord has a day. It is a day different from all other days, called "the Lord's day." In Mark 2:28 Jesus told us which day "the Lord's day" is. Notice carefully Jesus' words: *"The Son of man is Lord also of the Sabbath."* The Lord has a day, and that day is called the Sabbath by Jesus Himself.

Many people today believe that "the Lord's day" spoken of by John, and the "Sabbath" spoken of by Jesus, are two completely different days. But there is not a trace of evidence anywhere in Scripture to substantiate this belief. In fact, I believe you will discover from reading this book that "the Lord's day" *is* the "Sabbath" that was spoken of by Jesus.

But which day is the Sabbath? Let us turn in our Bibles to Exodus 20:8-11 and read the fourth commandment: *"Remember the Sabbath day, to keep it holy. Six days shalt thou labour, and do all thy work: But the seventh day is the Sabbath of the Lord thy God: in it thou shalt not do any work, thou, nor thy son, nor thy daughter, thy manservant, nor thy maidservant, nor thy cattle, nor thy stranger that is within thy gates: For in six days the Lord made heaven and earth, the sea, and all that in them is, and rested the seventh day: wherefore the Lord blessed the Sabbath day, and hallowed it."* The Sabbath, according to the fourth commandment, is the seventh day.

For those of you who believe that we are no longer bound by the Ten Commandment Law, please be patient.

We will discuss that issue in detail a little further along.

BEFORE WE GO FURTHER

Before we go any further in our discussion of the fourth commandment, let me say that obedience to a command, any command, is absolutely *meaningless* outside of a saved relationship with Jesus Christ. We are not saved by anything we can do. On the contrary, we are saved by faith alone through the grace and mercy of God. Yet the reality of that salvation generates in the heart of the converted person a desire to be obedient. Arnold Wallenkampf wrote that salvation inspires the born-again Christian "to believe what God says, to accept what God offers, and to do whatever God wishes, in gladhearted obedience." Arnold Wallenkamf, *Justified*, 1988, page 72.

While it's true that our good works will never *earn* us salvation, Scripture teaches that the absence of obedience may cause one to forfeit that salvation. If a person claims to have been justified by faith, and yet does not gradually begin to experience ethical change in his life, there is something radically wrong. While Ephesians 2:8 teaches that salvation comes by grace through faith alone, verse 10 tells us that salvation is *"unto good works."* This is another way of saying that the salvation experience produces the desire to be obedient in the heart of the born-again Christian.

Luther taught that while the believer is saved by faith, "he needs nothing further except to prove his faith by works." *Luther's Works*, Volume 35, page 367. Calvin's position was the same: "For we dream neither of a faith devoid of good works nor of a justification that stands without them." John Calvin, *Institutes*, Book 3, Chapter 16, Section 1. Charles Spurgeon wrote: "If it were possible for sin to be forgiven, and yet for the sinner to live just as he lived before, he would not really be saved." C. H. Spurgeon, *The Metropolitan Tabernacle Pulpit,* Volume 56, page 617. Behavior is the litmus test that proves

9

whether our salvation experience is genuine. 1 John 3:9 reads: *"No one who is born of God practices sin..." (New American Standard Bible).* And 1 John 2:3 says: *"And hereby we do know that we know Him, if we keep His commandments."*

Jesus expects His followers to bear fruit. In John 15:8 He said: *"Herein is my Father glorified, that ye bear much fruit; so shall ye be my disciples."* When we accept Jesus into our hearts, obedience will appear as fruitful evidence that we are connected to the True Vine (John 15:1-5). One must remember that a peach tree does not produce peaches *in order to be* a peach tree. Rather, it produces peaches because it *is* a peach tree. A Christian is not obedient *in order to be* saved. Rather, he is obedient because he *is* saved. Obedience must be the fruit, or the natural outgrowth of one's relationship with Jesus. Nathaniel Emmons said: "Obedience to God is the most infallible evidence of sincere and supreme love to Him." *Encyclopedia of Religious Quotations*, page 320.

It is with this understanding, that the honest Bible student cannot ignore the Biblical principle of obedience, that we launch into this study of the fourth commandment.

MOST COMMON QUESTIONS ABOUT THE SABBATH

Many Christians today believe that the Sabbath began with Moses at mount Sinai. **Did the Sabbath begin at mount Sinai, or is there evidence that the Sabbath existed before Sinai**?

Exodus 19:1 tells us that the Children of Israel came into the wilderness of Sinai in the *third month* after leaving Egypt. In other words, the Ten Commandments were not given to Moses on mount Sinai until at least *three months* after the Exodus. In Exodus 16:1 we are told that the Israelites were between Elim and Sinai in the Wilderness of Sin on the fifteenth day of the *second month* after leaving Egypt. It was while in this wilderness, two weeks before arriving at Sinai, that the Lord gave them manna. Follow along with me in Exodus 16:4,5: *"Then said the Lord unto Moses, Behold, I will rain bread from heaven for you; and the people shall go out and gather a certain rate every day, that I may prove them, whether they will walk in my law or no [not]. And it shall come to pass, that on the sixth day they shall prepare that which they bring in; and it shall be twice as much as they gather daily."*

The Israelites were only to gather a certain amount of manna each day. If they gathered too much, it would spoil by the next day (Exodus 16:19,20). But on the day before the Sabbath, they were to gather twice as much so that they would not have to gather manna on the Sabbath. Miraculously, this extra "Sabbath supply" did not spoil (Exodus 16:24).

Look with me at Exodus 16:22,23: *"And it came to pass, that on the sixth day they gathered twice as much bread, two omers for one man: and all the rulers of the congregation came and told Moses. And he said unto them, This is that which the Lord hath said, To morrow is the rest of the Holy Sabbath unto the Lord: bake that which ye will bake to day, and seethe that ye will seethe; and that which remaineth over lay up for you to be kept until the morning."* Verses 26-28 make this even more clear: *"Six days ye shall gather it; but on the seventh day, which is the Sabbath, in it there shall be none. And it came to pass, that there went out some of the people on the seventh day for to gather, and they found none. And the Lord said unto Moses, How long refuse ye to keep My commandments and My laws?"* It is obvious from these verses that the Sabbath and the Commandments were in place *before* the Israelites arrived at Sinai. Therefore, the Sabbath did not have its origin with God giving the tables of stone to Moses at mount Sinai.

Many people ask, **Isn't the Sabbath just for the Jews**? Turn with me to Genesis 2:1-3 and let us read: *"Thus the heavens and the earth were finished, and all the host of them. And on the seventh day God ended His work*

which He had made; and He rested on the seventh day from all His work which He had made. And God blessed the seventh day, and sanctified it: because that in it He had rested from all His work which God created and made."
The Sabbath was made at **creation**, 2000 years before there was a Jew. The Sabbath predates sin, pointing back to God as the Creator of a perfect world. The Sabbath was given to Adam, the father of the entire human race. Abraham is considered the father of the Jews (and he was a Gentile), so the Sabbath was made for all mankind, not just for the Jews.

Clifford Goldstein, in his book *A Pause For Peace,* 1992, page 51, uses a great illustration that I would like to share with you. It goes like this: "New Yorkers have been observing Christmas for years. Is, therefore, Christmas exclusively a New York holiday? Christmas predates New Yorkers, wasn't invented by New Yorkers, didn't start with New Yorkers, wasn't made specifically for New Yorkers, and is kept by others besides New Yorkers.

"The same with the Sabbath. It predates Jews, wasn't invented by Jews, didn't start with Jews, wasn't made specifically for Jews, and is kept by others besides Jews. Sabbath, therefore, no more belongs exclusively to Jews than Christmas does to the Big Apple."

The fourth commandment in Exodus 20:8-11 points back to the Sabbath of creation. The Hebrew words used in Exodus 20:11, which say that God "blessed" and "hallowed" the seventh day, come from the same root words used in Genesis 2 to say that God "blessed" and "sanctified" the seventh-day Sabbath after the creation of this earth. Both Exodus and Genesis use the Hebrew phrase *yom hassbi'i* for "the seventh day." Both use the same word for "made," *'sh* to describe God's creative activity. Also, the noun "Sabbath" in Exodus comes from the same Hebrew root *shbt*, meaning "to cease from labor" as used in Genesis to explain that God "rested" on the seventh day. There should be no doubt in our minds that the fourth commandment refers directly back to the cre-

12

ation Sabbath.

Eadie's Biblical Cyclopaedia, page 561 says: "It is not the Jewish Sabbath. There is no Jewish element, any more than there is in the third commandment, or the sixth." And L. F. Were wrote: "The Sabbath was not intended to be confined to Palestine, but being a spiritual institution, it is for all time, and for all people." Louis F. Were, *The Certainty of the Third Angel's Message,* pages 73,74.

Did Jesus keep the Sabbath? Look with me at Luke 4:16: *"And He came to Nazareth, where He had been brought up: and, as His **custom** was, He went into the synagogue on the Sabbath day, and stood up for to read."* (emphasis supplied). Now turn with me to Mark 6:2: *"And when the Sabbath day was come, He began to teach in the synagogue: and many hearing Him were astonished, saying, From whence hath this man these things? and what wisdom is this which is given unto Him, that even such mighty works are wrought by His hands?"* The Sabbath, established at Eden, was kept by patriarch, prophet, and the people of God throughout the centuries of pagan darkness. And when Christ came, at His incarnation, He likewise observed the same seventh day as the Sabbath. Jesus was in the habit of being in church on the Sabbath day.

Did the Apostles keep the Sabbath? Turn with me to Acts 13:42-44 and let's read: *"And when the Jews were gone out of the synagogue, the Gentiles besought that these words might be preached to them the next Sabbath. Now when the congregation was broken up, many of the Jews and religious proselytes followed Paul and Barnabas: who, speaking to them, persuaded them to continue in the grace of God. And the next Sabbath day came almost the whole city together to hear the word of God."* The disciples accompanied Jesus everywhere He went, and were present when He taught on the Sabbath in Mark 6 and Luke 4. Now these very same disciples were teaching in the synagogue on the Sabbath, **after** Jesus had ascended to heaven. I will discuss in more detail this issue of the apostles and the Sabbath in the section entitled, "The Sabbath in the New Testament."

Since the Bible does not differentiate between "the Lord's day" and the "seventh-day Sabbath," **Which day is the seventh day**? *Webster's Standard Dictionary* says: "Saturday is the seventh day of the week."

At this point many people ask, **How do you know that Saturday is still the seventh day of the week**? **How do you know that the Sabbath hasn't been lost over the years**?

HAS THE SABBATH BEEN LOST?

There is no need to carry the question of "lost time" back before the Christian era. Any knowledgable person will agree that the weekly cycle, which had its origin at creation, was still employed in Palestine at the time of Christ. All Sundaykeeping people believe that Christ rose from the tomb on the first day of the week, which we call "Sunday." Now, the Bible plainly states that the day preceding that first day of the week was *"the Sabbath day according to the commandment."* (read Luke 23:56-24:1). Jesus was accustomed to keeping the Sabbath, as we just read in Luke 4:16. Thus the seventh day in the weekly cycle in the first century of the Christian Era was the same "seventh day" of the Sabbath commandment. Therefore it is quite unnecessary to present evidence for "lost time" for the centuries that preceded our Lord Jesus Christ. But for those who would feel more comfortable being able to trace the Sabbath right back to the beginning of time, I hope that the following information will be helpful.

God created **Adam** on the sixth day of creation week. His first full day of life was that very same seventh-day Sabbath which God pronounced to be *"blessed"* and *"sanctified"* on that last day of creation (Genesis 2:1-3). Adam spent that first Sabbath, not working, but celebrating with his Maker the inauguration of the completed and perfect creation. He stood face to face with God when God pronounced that first Sabbath to be "holy time." Psalms 119:172 says: *"All thy commandments are righteousness..."* Adam's son, **Abel** was called "righteous" by Jesus (Matthew 23:35), so we know that he kept God's commandments, which included the Sabbath. **Enoch** "walked with God," (Genesis 5:24); Noah was a "preacher of righteousness" (2 Peter 2:5); **Abraham** commanded his household to "keep the way of the Lord" (Genesis 18:19), so we know that they kept God's commandments. In Palestinian literature, frequent mention is made of Abraham, Jacob, and Joseph as scrupulous Sabbathkeepers. Jacob's children (Israel) became slaves in Egypt, and, through slavery, lost their knowledge of spiritual things before **Moses** led them out of Egypt at the Exodus. In the wilderness God showed Israel which day the Sabbath was through the miracle of the **manna** (Exodus 16:4-8). At **Sinai** God gave the Ten Commandments and asked Israel to *"Remember the Sabbath day to keep it holy."* Under the strict Mosaic system, the Sabbath could not have been lost from Sinai to the time of **Jesus**, who kept the Sabbath as His *"custom"* (Luke 4:16).

Let's summarize what you have just read. If the Sabbath had been lost between the time of Adam and Moses, God would have rectified it at Sinai with the Ten Commandments. If the Sabbath had been lost between the time of Moses and Jesus, Jesus would have rectified it when He was here on earth. It is very easy to trace the Sabbath from before the time of Christ to our present day as you will discover from reading the next few pages.

HAS THE CALENDAR BEEN CHANGED?

Many people are surprised to find that Saturday is the Bible Sabbath. One question they most often ask is, **How do you know that Saturday is the same day that Jesus kept**? **How do you know that the calendar hasn't been changed**?

Julius Caesar authorized a calendar (known as the

Julian Calendar) which was calculated by the Greek astronomer Sosigenes. It went into effect in 45 B.C. and was used until A.D. 1582. But because the Julian Calendar was imperfect, it was reformed in A.D. 1582 by Pope Gregory XIII. Since then, our calendar has been known as the Gregorian Calendar. It is important that you understand that there have only been two calendars since *before the time of Christ* to our present day—the Julian from **45 B.C.** (some 40 years before Christ's birth) and the Gregorian from A.D. 1582.

The computations of Sosigenes made the year a bit too lengthy, and by the time of Pope Gregory XIII the Julian Calendar had drifted ten (10) days away from the seasons. The spring equinox fell on March 11 rather than March 21. To correct this, and to bring the calendar year back into harmony with the solar year, ten days were dropped from the calendar. But they were dropped only from the number of days in the *month*, not from the number of days in the *week*. Here is the calendar from October of A.D. 1582 when that calendar change was made:

October 1582 AD

Sn	Mn	Tu	Wd	Th	Fr	St
	1	2	3	4	15	16
17	18	19	20	21	22	23
24	25	26	27	28	29	30
31						

You will notice that the ten days were dropped between Thursday the 4th and Friday the 15th. You will also notice that the weekly cycle was not changed. In other words, Friday still followed Thursday, Saturday still followed Friday, etc. *The Encyclopedia Americana*, 1973 Edition, Vol. 5, p. 188, says of this calendar change: "Note that the continuity of the days of the week was maintained." *The Catholic Encyclopedia* also tells us that the weekly cycle was not altered. In Vol. 9, p. 251 it says: "Every imaginable proposition was made, only one idea was never mentioned, the abandonment of the seven day week." We are on the same weekly cycle that Jesus was on!

James Robertson, Director of the U.S. Naval Observatory, Department of the Navy, Washington, D.C., wrote: "We have had occasion to investigate the results of the works of specialists in chronology and we have never found one of them that has ever had the slightest doubt about the continuity of the weekly cycle since long before the Christian era." Quoted by Francis D. Nichol, *Answers to Objections,* page 560.

Frank W. Dyson, Astronomer Royal of Great Britain, Royal Observatory, Greenwich, London, wrote: "As far as I know, in the various changes of the Calendar there has been no change in the seven day rota of the week, which has come down from very early times." *Ibid*, page 562.

The change to the Gregorian Calendar was made only in Spain, Portugal, and Italy in 1582. The British countries refused to make the change when the Pope ordered it, so they continued with the old Julian Calendar until the year A.D. 1752. By that time, it was necessary to drop eleven (11) days. Here is the calendar for September of that year when the British adopted the Gregorian Calendar:

September 1752 AD

Sn	Mn	Tu	Wd	Th	Fr	St
		1	2	14	15	16
17	18	19	20	21	22	23
24	25	26	27	28	29	30

You will notice that the eleven days were dropped between Wednesday the 2nd and Thursday the 14th. You will also notice that while their days of the month had been different from the Gregorian Calendar, their days of the *week* were exactly the same. In other words, Saturday was the same day under both the Julian and Gregorian calendars, proof once again that the weekly cycle has remained

17

constant.

The following statement can be found in the *Catholic Encyclopedia,* Volume 3, page 740, Article, "Chronology." It reads: "It is to be noted that in the Christian period the order of days of the week has never been interrupted."

In Russia, the change to the Gregorian Calendar was not made until the year 1918. By then the two calendars were thirteen (13) days apart, yet Saturday in Russia was exactly the same day of the week as Saturday in every other part of the world. Today in Russia, their Saturday is our Saturday, proof that the *weekly cycle* has not been changed.

The Greek Catholic Church did not adopt the Gregorian reform until 1923. But when it was Saturday in Greece, it was Saturday in every other part of the world, proof once again that the weekly cycle of days has not been altered. But that's not all! There is more proof that the day we call Saturday is the seventh-day Sabbath. In 108 languages of the world, "Saturday" is rendered "Sabbath." For example:

Spanish	"Sabado"
Italian	"Sabbato"
Portuguese	"Sabbado"
Latin	"Sabbatum"
Bulgarian	"Shubbuta"
Russian	"Subbota"
Arabic	"As-Sabt"
Greek	"Sabbaton"

Linguistic evidence shows that different peoples, in widely-scattered parts of the world, have always called Saturday by the name of "Sabbath."

Samuel M. Zwemer, D.D., a former professor at Princeton University, and long known authority on Mohammedanism, wrote: "The only time reckoning on which Christians, Moslems, and Jews agree is that of the days of the week. [In Mohammedanism] these are num-

18

bered and called by their numbers, save Friday and Saturday, which are known as the 'day of the assembling' and the 'day of the Sabbath.'" *The United Presbyterian*, September 26, 1929.

If one still has doubts as to Saturday being the seventh day and Sunday being the first day of the week, just ask any Sundaykeeping church which day of the week Easter falls on. They will tell you that Easter is the celebration of Christ's resurrection on the first day of the week (Mark 16:9). Sunday is not the Bible seventh-day Sabbath. Sunday is without a doubt the first day of the week.

DID JESUS CHANGE THE SABBATH?

One question I am always asked is, **"If Saturday is the seventh-day Sabbath, why do most Christians keep Sunday, the first day of the week? Didn't Jesus change the Sabbath from Saturday to Sunday**?"

The answer to that question is "no." There is absolutely no record anywhere in Scripture where the Sabbath was changed from the seventh day to the first day of the week. In fact, the first day of the week is mentioned only *eight times* in the entire New Testament. If Jesus had done something so important as to change one of His Ten Commandments, don't you think He would have told us? Let's take a look at each of these eight texts that mention the first day of the week in the New Testament:

> **Matthew 28:1** *"In the end of the Sabbath, as it began to dawn toward the first day of the week, came Mary Magdalene and the other Mary to see the sepulchre."*

Many Christians believe that Matthew 28:1 is the *exact point* in Scripture where the change of the Sabbath was made by Jesus. But if one examines the facts carefully, it is easy to see that that is not what the verse is saying.

The Greek word *opse* here translated "end," may mean

either "late" or "after." In Hebrew reckoning the day ended at sunset. This means that the Sabbath ended when the sun set on Saturday evening, which is consistent with Matthew's use of *opse* in this verse. It was *"In the end of* [or after] *the Sabbath, as it began to dawn toward the first day..."* (meaning at sunrise on Sunday morning), when the two Marys went to the tomb.

That Matthew's use of *opse* is intended to mean "after the Sabbath was over" is confirmed by the other three Gospel writers in defining the time when the women came to the tomb. Mark says plainly: "when the Sabbath was past" (Mark 16:1). Luke wrote: "the first day of the week, very early in the morning" (Luke 24:1). John says: "the first day of the week...when it was yet dark" (John 20:1). Friedrich Blass, Ph.D., Th.D., Litt.D., in his book, *Grammar of New Testament Greek*, page 97, confirms the fact that the Sabbath was "clearly over" when the women came to the sepulcher on Sunday morning. This means that Sunday is not the Bible Sabbath, but the day *after* the Sabbath.

The word for "Sabbath" in Matthew 28:1, and the word for "week" are translated from the same identical Greek word *sabbaton*. By an idiom of the language, both the singular and the plural form of *sabbaton* can be used for either "Sabbath" or "week." One must study the context of the entire verse to know how to correctly translate. A rule to remember in Greek is that all modifying adjectives must agree in gender, as well as in case and number, with the noun they modify. When context warrants *sabbaton* to be translated "Sabbath," Louw and Nida's *Greek-English Lexicon of the New Testament* states that it means "The seventh or last day of the week, Sabbath, Saturday." And when context warrants the translation of "week," it means "a period of seven days" or "the period of time that falls between two Sabbaths."

Some students of Scripture, wishing to promote Sunday sacredness, have translated Matthew 28:1 as saying that at Jesus' death, "the first day of the week" became the seventh-day Sabbath, or the "first" in a series of new sabbaths. They argue that the phrase "the first day of the week" should read "the first of the sabbaths," and they conclude that Matthew here designates resurrection Sunday as the first occasion on which Sabbath sacredness was transferred to the first day of the week. But such a translation is grammatically impossible in the Greek. The word *sabbaton* is neuter in gender, and *first* is feminine. Hence to make *first* mean *first Sabbath* would violate the most fundamental and invariable rule in Greek inflection—that all modifying adjectives must agree with the noun they modify. Hence the true meaning of the phrase is perfectly expressed in its translation "the first day of the week."

No knowledgeable Greek scholar has ever attempted to make an argument in favor of Sunday sacredness on the basis of this syntax error. In fact, Greek Professor, Dr. Wilbur Fletcher Steele, in an article published in the *Methodist Review*, May-June, 1899, wrote that this argument for Sunday sacredness "rests upon the profoundest ignoring or ignorance of a law of syntax fundamental to inflected speech." He called this misuse of *sabbaton* a "travestied exegesis" and a "monumental blunder." His article was entitled, "Must Syntax Die That Sunday May Live?" Greek scholar, F.D. Nichol, wrote: "Novices who have made such an attempt have been rebuked by their more scholarly Sundaykeeping brethren who categorically deny the possibility of such a translation."

Matthew 28:1 makes the simple statement that the two Marys went to the tomb *after* the Sabbath was over, as the sun was rising early on Sunday morning. Do not try to complicate Matthew's statement by reading more into it than this.

> **Mark 16:2** *"And very early in the morning the first day of the week, they came unto the sepulchre at the rising of the sun."*

In the Gospels each of the four evangelists gives his

21

own account of the rapid and dramatic events of the resurrection morning. In view of the fact that Luke speaks of the bringing of spices to embalm Jesus' body (Luke 24:1) after the Sabbath was over, it is inconceivable to suppose that Mark is here referring to Sunday sacredness while Luke was referring to Sunday in terms of a work day.

Do not try to read anything into this verse that is not there. Mark 16:2 is synoptic (sharing a common view) with Matthew 28:1, and it simply states that "they" went to the tomb as the sun was coming up on Sunday morning.

> **Mark 16:9** *"Now when Jesus was risen early the first day of the week, He appeared first to Mary Magdalene, out of whom He had cast seven devils."*

Christ rose early the first day of the week, but there is no record anywhere that He blessed that day. On the other hand, He did *"bless"* the seventh-day Sabbath and *"sanctified"* it at creation (Genesis 2:3). "Sanctified" comes from the Hebrew *qadash* which means to "consecrate" or "dedicate" or "appoint." "Sanctify" in the Greek means to "consecrate" to "make holy," or to "venerate." *The Random House Dictionary* says "venerate" means "to regard or treat with reverence."

> **Luke 24:1** *"Now upon the first day of the week, very early in the morning, they came unto the sepulchre, bringing the spices which they had prepared, and certain others with them."*

By reading the last three verses of Luke 23, one can see that those who laid Christ in the grave on Friday evening returned home and rested on the Sabbath, *"according to the commandment."* They returned on Sunday morning to do the work of anointing the body. This is consistent with what Matthew wrote in Matthew 28:1. There is not the least basis here for Sunday holiness. In

22

fact, Christ Himself kept the commandment in His death by resting on the Sabbath. Many people try to make Luke 24:1 prove Sunday sacredness when that's not what it's saying at all.

> **John 20:1** *"The first day of the week cometh Mary Magdalene early, when it was yet dark, unto the sepulchre, and seeth the stone taken away from the sepulchre."*

This verse is synoptic with the previous four verses that we have already discussed. And once again, it is easy to see that there is nothing in this text that could possibly suggest a change in the Sabbath from the seventh day to the first day of the week.

> **John 20:19** *"Then the same day at evening, being the first day of the week, when the doors were shut where the disciples were assembled for fear of the Jews, came Jesus and stood in the midst, and saith unto them, Peace be unto you."*

Many Christians use this verse to say that Jesus' followers worshipped on Sunday in honor of the resurrection. But that is *not* what the verse is saying. After the disciples discovered that Jesus' body was not in the tomb, they locked themselves up (probably in the same upper room where they had just eaten the last supper with Jesus) out of fear for their own lives, not to keep a new Sabbath on the first day of the week. The key expression in this verse is *"for fear of the Jews."* Except for Mary's testimony, the disciples didn't even know for a certainty that Jesus had actually risen. All they knew was that His body was no longer in the tomb. Not until He appeared, showing them *"His hands and His side"* (verse 20) did they know for sure that He had risen from the dead. Locked doors hardly sounds like a religious service to me. The doors were locked because the disciples were afraid that the Jews were going to do to them what they had just done to their Master.

John's silence on the sanctity of the first day remains significant because the Gospel of John was written at the end of the first century. John wrote his gospel in the year A.D. 97, after he wrote Revelation in A.D. 96. This was nearly 70 years after Jesus' crucifixion and resurrection. If the first day had been made a holy day in place of the seventh day, don't you think John would have alluded to it somewhere in his gospel? I believe he was silent on the subject of Sunday sacredness because he knew nothing of it.

> **Acts 20:7** *"And upon the first day of the week, when the disciples came together to break bread, Paul preached unto them, ready to depart on the morrow; and continued his speech until midnight."*

The account of creation in Genesis tells us that the dark part of the day comes before the light part of the day. It says: *"...and the evening and the morning were the first day, ...and the evening and the morning were the second day, ...and the evening and the morning were the third day,"* etc. Time was calculated from sunset to sunset. When the sun went down, a new day began. This is the reason for the Sabbath in the Bible beginning at sundown on Friday, the preparation day, and continuing until sundown on Saturday, the Sabbath. Leviticus 23:32 tells us that the Sabbath is to be kept from *"even to even."* After the sun sets on the Sabbath, the first day of the week begins. Paul was actually preaching a Saturday night meeting here in Acts 20:7. The text says that he continued to preach clear up until midnight. *The New English Bible* actually translates this "Saturday night." Verses 8-11 of Acts 20 continue: *"And there were many lights in the upper chamber, where they were gathered together. And there sat in a window a certain young man named Eutychus, being fallen into a deep sleep: and as Paul was long preaching, he sunk down with sleep, and fell down from the third loft, and was taken up dead. And Paul went down, and fell on him, and embracing him said, Trouble not yourselves; for his life is in him. When he therefore was come up again, and had broken bread, and eaten, and talked a long while, even till break of day, so he departed."* Paul preached until midnight Saturday night, raised Eutychus from the dead, talked and ate with the disciples until the sun came up, and then departed on Sunday morning to catch a ship. There is no support here for the observance of the first day of the week as a holy day.

Many people try to reason that because Paul broke bread with the disciples here in Acts 20:7, that it means that they had communion on Sunday. Don't forget that this meeting took place on the dark part of the first day, which was actually Saturday night. The "breaking of bread" does not set a precedence for Sunday sacredness. Acts 2:46 says: *"And they, continuing **daily** with one accord in the temple, and breaking bread from house to house, did eat their meat with gladness and singleness of heart."* (emphasis supplied). They broke bread every day! This means that they ate together and fellowshipped with one another every day. Breaking of bread in no way makes a holy day out of the first day of the week.

>   **1 Corinthians 16:2** *"Upon the first day of the week let every one of you lay by him in store, as God hath prospered him, that there be no gatherings when I come."*

All Paul is saying here is that if his listeners would lay their offerings *"in store"* at the beginning of the week, they wouldn't have to be bothered with gathering them together when he got there to speak. Most of us will have to admit that we would have nothing left at the end of the week for church if we waited until then to lay aside our tithes and offerings. What Paul is saying is, "Lay it aside first, at the beginning of the week so that you won't have to be troubled with gathering it together when I come." The phrase *"by him in store"* is significant. *"By him"* comes from the Greek *par'heauto,* or "by himself." The English equivalent would be "at home." *"In store"* means literally "treasuring up" or "storing up," probably in some special place in the home.

How do I know that Paul kept the Sabbath? Acts 17:2 says: *"And Paul, as his **manner** was, went in unto them, and three Sabbath days reasoned with them out of the scriptures."* (emphasis supplied). Some people try to argue that Paul kept Sunday. Not true! If Paul had kept Sunday in place of the Sabbath, the Jewish converts to Christianity would have accused him of Sabbath-breaking. This they *never* did. The Jews constantly accused Jesus of Sabbath-breaking because He didn't keep it the way *they* thought it should be kept. But nowhere in Scripture was Paul ever accused of breaking the Bible Sabbath. Had he done so he could never have escaped the accusations of the Jews.

Not one of these eight New Testament texts that we just studied supports the changing of the Bible Sabbath to Sunday. The Sabbath was made by the act of God resting from creation on the seventh day, and "blessing" and "sanctifying" that day. That act was announced to mankind by the voice of God Himself from Sinai. That divine command has never with equal formality been abolished. There has never been a comparable enactment making Sunday the Christian Sabbath. Until such a legislative act by God sanctifying the first day of the week is produced, I maintain that nothing whatsoever can possibly change the decree of Almighty God.

WHY DO SOME KEEP SUNDAY?

If Saturday is the Bible Sabbath, **Where did Sunday observance come from**? Long before there was a Protestant religion, long before the reformers (Huss, Wycliff, Luther, etc.) protested and broke away from the Catholic Church, the Sabbath observance was changed from Saturday to Sunday. Notice this statement found in *Neander's Church History*, Johann Neander, translated by Henry John Rose, page 186: "The festival of Sunday, like all other festivals, was always only a human ordinance, and it was far from the intentions of the apostles to establish a divine command in this respect; far from them, and from the early apostolic church, to transfer the laws of the Sabbath to Sunday. Perhaps, at the end of the second century a false application of this kind had begun to take place; for men appear by that time to have considered laboring on Sunday as a sin."

The Catholic Church claims to have made this change, as can be seen from their publication *The Catholic Mirror*, September, 1893: "The Catholic Church for over one thousand years before the existence of a Protestant, by virtue of her divine mission, changed the day from Saturday to Sunday." What follows are additional acknowledgements about the change of the Sabbath by Roman Catholic authors:

CATHOLIC ACKNOWLEDGEMENTS

"**Question**: How prove you that the Church hath power to command feasts and holy days?
Answer: By the very act of changing the Sabbath into Sunday, which Protestants allow of; and therefore they fondly contradict themselves, by keeping Sunday strictly and breaking most other feasts commanded by the same Church." H. Tuberville, *An Abridgement of Christian Doctrine*, page 58.

"**Question**: Is the observance of Sunday as the day of rest a matter clearly laid down in Scripture?
Answer: It certainly is not; and yet all Protestants consider the observance of this particular day as essentially necessary to salvation. To say we observe the Sunday because

Christ rose from the dead on that day, is to say we act without warrant of Scripture; and we might as well say that we should rest on Thursday, because Christ ascended to heaven on that day, and rested in reality from the work of redemption." Dr. Stephen Keenan, *The Controversial Catechism*, page 160.

"**Question**: Have you any other way of proving that the Church has power to institute festivals of precept?
Answer: Had she not such power, she could not have done that in which all modern religionists agree with her—she could not have substituted the observance of Sunday, the first day of the week, for the observance of Saturday, the seventh day—a change for which there is no Scriptural authority." Dr. Stephen Keenan, *A Doctrinal Catechism*, 3rd Edition, page 174.

"**Question**: Which is the Sabbath day?
Answer: Saturday is the Sabbath.
Question: Why do we observe Sunday instead of Saturday?
Answer: We observe Sunday instead of Saturday because the Catholic Church in the council of Laodicea [A.D. 336] transferred the solemnity from Saturday to Sunday." Peter Geiermann, *The Convert's Catechism of Catholic Doctrine*, 1934, page 50.

The Sabbath was not changed by God; it was changed by man only decades after the death of John the Revelator. But who gave man the right to change one of God's Commandments? Jesus Himself said that not *"one jot or tittle"* could be changed in the law until heaven and earth pass away (Matthew 5:17-19).
   So what is Sunday observance based on? Tradition! And what did Jesus have to say about tradition? Matthew 15:3 says: *"But He answered and said unto them, Why do ye also transgress the commandment of God by your tradition?"* And then in verse 9 He said: *"But in **vain** they*

28

do worship me, teaching for doctrines the commandments of men." (emphasis supplied). The word "vain" here comes from the Greek *matane* which means, "to no purpose, unsuccessful." Jesus is saying, "There's no purpose to your worship if you teach man's commandments in place of My commandments."

The following statement can be found in the official Catholic publication *Our Sunday Visitor*, June 11, 1950: "In all their official books of instruction Protestants claim that their religion is based on the Bible and the Bible only, and they reject tradition as even a part of their rule of faith... There is no place in the New Testament where it is distinctly stated that Christ changed the day of worship from Saturday to Sunday. Yet, all Protestants follow tradition in observing Sunday."

This statement was found in the Catholic publication *Question Box*, 1915, page 179: "If the Bible is the only guide for the Christian then the Seventh-day Adventist is right, in observing the Saturday with the Jew... Is it not strange, that those [Sunday keeping Protestants] who make the Bible their only teacher, should inconsistently follow in this matter the tradition of the Catholic Church."

Here is a statement that appeared in *The Catholic Mirror*, December 23, 1893: "Reason and sense demand the acceptance of one or the other of these alternatives; either Protestantism and the keeping holy of Saturday, or Catholicity and the keeping holy of Sunday. Compromise is impossible."

Cardinal Gibbons wrote in *The Faith Of Our Fathers*, 92nd Edition, page 89: "You may read the Bible from Genesis to Revelation, and you will not find a single line authorizing the sanctification of Sunday. The Scriptures enforce the religious observance of Saturday, a day which we never sanctify."

The Catholic Virginian, October 3, 1947 said: "Nowhere in the Bible do we find that Christ or the apostles ordered that the Sabbath be changed from Saturday to Sunday. We have the commandment of God given to

Moses to keep holy the Sabbath day, that is the seventh day of the week, Saturday. Today most Christians keep Sunday because it has been revealed to us by the Church outside the Bible."

The New Catholic Encyclopedia, Volume 12, page 781, says: "Nothing in the comportment of Jesus gave the slightest hint that he would have considered it preferable to transfer the Sabbath observance to any other day."

Father Segur, in *Plain Talk About Protestantism*, page 213, wrote: "The observance of Sunday by the Protestants is an homage they pay, in spite of themselves, to the authority of the Catholic Church."

Not only do Catholic authors admit that their church changed the Sabbath, Protestant authors have made the same acknowledgements.

PROTESTANT ACKNOWLEDGEMENTS
BAPTIST

"There was never any formal or authoritative change from the Jewish seventh-day Sabbath to the Christian first day observance." William Owen Carver, *The Lord's Day In Our Day*, page 49.

"Of course, I quite well know that Sunday did come into use in early Christian history as a religious day, as we learn from the Christian Fathers and other sources. But what a pity that it comes branded with the mark of paganism, and christened with the name of the sun god, when adopted and sanctioned by the papal apostasy, and bequeathed as a sacred legacy to Protestantism!" Dr. Edward T. Hiscox, author of *The Baptist Manual*, in a paper read before a New York ministers' conference held November 16, 1890, quoted by Mark Finley, *The Almost Forgotten Day,* page 106.

"The Early Church celebrated the first day of the week as the Lord's day, but to many people the Sabbath is Saturday, which is in the Old Testament Scriptures." Dr. Billy Graham, *Decision*, April 1989, page 2.

CONGREGATIONALIST

"It must be confessed that there is no law in the New Testament concerning the first day." *Buck's Theological Dictionary*, page 403.

"There is no command in the Bible requiring us to observe the first day of the week as the Christian Sabbath." Orin Fowler, A.M., *Mode and Subjects of Baptism*.

"The current notion that Christ and His apostles authoritatively substituted the first day for the seventh, is absolutely without any authority in the New Testament." Dr. Lyman Abbott, *Christian Union*, January 19, 1882.

"The Christian Sabbath [Sunday] is not in the Scriptures, and was not by the primitive church called the Sabbath." *Dwight's Theology*, Volume 4, page 401.

"It is quite clear that, however rigidly or devoutly we may spend Sunday, we are not keeping the Sabbath... The Sabbath was founded on a specific, divine command. We can plead no such command for the obligation to observe Sunday... There is not a single sentence in the New Testament to suggest that we incur any penalty by violating the supposed sanctity of Sunday." R. W. Dale, D.D., *The Ten Commandments*, London: Hodder and Stoughton, pages 106,107.

EPISCOPAL

"Not any ecclesiastical writer of the first three centuries attributed the origin of Sunday observance either to Christ or to His apostles." Sir William Domville, *Examination Of The Six Texts*, pages 6,7 (Supplement).

"Where are we told in Scripture that we are to keep the first day at all? We are commanded to keep the seventh; but we are nowhere commanded to keep the first day... The reason why we keep the first day of the week holy instead of the seventh is for the same reason that we observe many other things, not because the Bible, but because the church has enjoined it." Isaac Williams, D.D., *Plain Sermons On The Catechism*, Volume 1, pages 334-336.

"The Bible commandment says on the seventh day

thou shalt rest. That is Saturday. Nowhere in the Bible is it laid down that worship should be done on Sunday." Phillip Carrington, *Toronto Daily Star*, October 26, 1949.

CHURCH OF ENGLAND

"The seventh day of the week has been deposed from its title to obligatory religious observance, and its prerogative has been carried over to the first, under no direct precept of Scripture." William E. Gladstone, *Later Gleanings,* page 342.

"There is no word, no hint, in the New Testament about abstaining from work on Sunday... Into the rest of Sunday no divine law enters... The observance of Ash Wednesday or Lent stands on exactly the same footing as the observance of Sunday." Canon Eyton, *Ten Commandments,* pages 62,63,65.

Dr. Peter Heylyn, a Church of England historian wrote: "The Saturday is called amongst them by no other name than that which formerly it had, the Sabbath. So that whenever, for a thousand years and upwards, we meet with *Sabbatum* in any writer of what name soever, it must be understood of no day but Saturday." Peter Heylyn, *History of the Sabbath*, Part 2, Chapter 2, Section 12.

LUTHERAN

"The observance of the Lord's day [Sunday] is founded not on any command of God, but on the authority of the Church." Augsburg Confession Of Faith, quoted in *The Catholic Sabbath Manual*, Part 2, Chapter 1, Section 10.

"The seventh day He [God] did sanctify for Himself. This had the special purpose of making us understand that the seventh day in particular should be devoted to divine worship. Although man lost his knowledge of God, nevertheless God wanted this commandment about sanctifying the Sabbath to remain in force." Martin Luther, Comments on Genesis 2:3, *Luther's Works*.

"They [the popes] allege the change of the Sabbath into the Lord's day, contrary, as it seemeth, to the Decalogue;

and they have no example more in their mouths than the change of the Sabbath. They will needs have the church's power to be very great, because it hath dispensed with a precept of the Decalogue." Philip Schaff quoting Martin Luther, *The Creeds of Christendom*, Volume 3, page 64.

METHODIST

"Take the matter of Sunday. There are indications in the New Testament as to how the church came to keep the first day as its day of worship, but there is no passage telling Christians to keep that day, or to transfer the Jewish Sabbath to that day." Harris Franklin Rall, *Christian Advocate*, July 2, 1949.

"The reason we observe the first day instead of the seventh is based on no positive command. One will search the Scriptures in vain for authority for changing from the seventh day to the first." Clovis G. Chappell, *Ten Rules for Living*, page 61.

"It is true there is no positive command for infant baptism...nor is there any for keeping holy the first day of the week." Dr. Binney, M.E., *Theological Compendium,* page 103.

"There is no intimation here that the Sabbath was done away with or that its moral use was superseded, by the introduction of Christianity." Adam Clarke, *The New Testament of Our Lord and Savior Jesus Christ*, New York, Volume 2, page 524.

MOODY BIBLE INSTITUTE

"The Sabbath was binding in Eden and it has been in force ever since. This fourth commandment begins with the word, 'Remember,' showing that the Sabbath already existed when God wrote the law on the tables of stone at Sinai. How can men claim that this one commandment has been done away with when they will admit that the other nine are still binding?" Dwight L. Moody, *Weighed and Wanting*, page 47.

"We have abundant evidence both in the New Testament and in the early history of the church to prove that gradually Sunday came to be observed instead of the Jewish Sabbath, apart from any specific commandment." Norman C. Deck, *Moody Bible Institute Monthly*, November, 1936, page 138.

PRESBYTERIAN

"The Sabbath is a part of the decalogue, the Ten Commandments. This alone forever settles the question as to the perpetuity of the institution... Until, therefore, it can be shown that the whole Moral Law has been repealed, the Sabbath will stand... The teaching of Christ confirms the perpetuity of the Sabbath." T.C. Blake D.D., *Theology Condensed*, pages 474,475.

"God instituted the Sabbath at the creation of man, setting apart the seventh day for that purpose, and imposed its observance, as a universal and perpetual moral obligation upon the race." Dr. Archibald Hodges, Tract No. 175 of the Presbyterian Board of Publication.

How incredible! These frank statements, coming from both Catholics and Protestants who worship on Sunday, show the extremely shaky foundation on which Sunday observance rests. You might ask, "How can this be?" And the best answer I can give you is a story told by Mark Finley. It goes like this:

"One day during the time of Imperial Russia, the Czar was walking through one of the beautiful parks connected with his palace. He came upon a sentry standing guard near a patch of shrubs. Surprised to find a guard in that place, he inquired, 'What are you doing?' 'I don't know,' answered the sentry. 'I am following the captain's orders.' The Czar asked the captain, 'Why do you have a sentry standing guard over a patch of shrubs?' 'Regulations have always been that way,' the captain responded, 'but I don't know the reason for it.' After a thorough investigation, the Czar discovered that nobody in his court could remember a time when it had not been that way. So the Czar turned to the archives containing the ancient records and, to his surprise, this is what he discovered. One hundred years before, Catherine The Great ordered a rose bush to be planted and had stationed a sentry nearby so that no one would trample on the young plant. The plant had long since died. Now a guard stood watching, but he didn't know what he was guarding." Quoted by Mark A. Finley, The *Almost Forgotten Day*, 1988, pages 31,32.

We just read the statement from *The Catholic Mirror* which says: "The Catholic Church, for over one thousand years before the existence of a Protestant, by virtue of her divine mission, changed the day from Saturday to Sunday." A thousand years before a Protestant even existed the change was made, and yet scores of Protestant churches are still standing guard over that "rose bush" today. They are believing, defending, and guarding a doctrine that has slipped into the church through tradition. They are guarding this doctrine while most of their members know nothing of its origin.

"The Protestant world, at its birth, found the Christian Sabbath [Sunday] too strongly entrenched to run counter to its existence... The Christian Sabbath is therefore, to this day, the acknowledged offspring of the Catholic church." *The Catholic Mirror*, September 23, 1893.

ORIGIN OF SUNDAY OBSERVANCE

It may come as a surprise to you to learn that not one Christian started keeping Sunday as a day of religious rest until long after the ascension of Jesus. It's a well documented fact that the first Christians to abandon the Sabbath for Sunday were those in Alexandria and Rome.

During the first century A.D. well over one hundred thousand Jews and Christians were put to death by Rome. Nero was especially ruthless, and in fact it was he who had the apostle Paul beheaded. The persecution of the Jews was so great during this time that Christians began trying to distance themselves from Judaism. This Jewish persecution by Rome seems to have created the desire among Christians to be viewed as different from the Jews, in the hope that Rome would then stop persecuting them. This desire to disassociate Christianity from Judaism brought on the rejection of the Sabbath and the subsequent substitution of a new day of worship. Christian Sunday observance originated in Rome during the second century, rather than in Jerusalem during the time of the apostles, as many people believe.

"Opposition to Judaism introduced the particular festival of Sunday very early, indeed, into the place of the Sabbath." Johann Neander, *General History of the Christian Religion and Church*, (Rose's translation), page 186.

Dr. Samuele Bacchiocchi wrote: "Anti-Judaism appears to have caused a widespread devaluation and repudiation of the Sabbath." Samuele Bacchiocchi, *From Sabbath To Sunday,* 1977, Pontifical Gregorian University Press, page 269.

Mark Finley wrote: "It was Sixtus, the bishop of the Christian church in Rome, who began the process that led to a transference of the day of worship from the Sabbath to Sunday. He convinced Christians to celebrate the resurrection, which occured on Sunday... At first the celebration was not a weekly observance but an annual one. By changing this celebration to Sunday and applying it to the resurrection, the Christians in Rome were able to disassociate themselves from the Jews.

"It just so happened that this resurrection celebration coincided with a joyous Roman festival in honor of the sun. The converted sun worshiper felt very much at home with the Christian spring festival, held on the sun's day, to honor the resurrection. Thus Sixtus, by encouraging Christians to celebrate the resurrection on the first day, actually put them in the position of honoring the sun's day." Mark A. Finley, *The Almost Forgotten Day*, 1988, pages 46,47.

"Until the Second Century there is no concrete evidence of a Christian weekly Sunday celebration anywhere. The first specific references during that century come from Alexandria and Rome, places that also early rejected the observance of the seventh-day Sabbath." Dr. Kenneth A. Strand, *The Sabbath in Scripture and History*, page 330.

Socrates wrote: "Almost all churches throughout the world celebrate the sacred mysteries [communion] on the Sabbath of every week, yet the Christians of Alexandria and at Rome...refuse to do this." Socrates Scholasticus, *Ecclesiastical History*, Book 5, Chapter 22, page 404.

"This drift into compromise in order to win the pagans was accented by the first civil Sunday law in A.D. 321, passed by the emperor of Rome, Constantine [a former sun-worshiper]. It was one of his first official acts following his nominal acceptance of Christianity, when he put himself under the spiritual direction of the Roman Catholic clergy and 'made the priests of God his counselors.'" Eusebius, *Life of Constantine*, Book 1, Chapter 32, cited in *Nicene and Post-Nicene Fathers*, Second Series, Volume 1, page 491.

"The earliest recognition of the observance of Sunday as a legal duty is a constitution of Constantine in A.D. 321, enacting that all courts of justice, inhabitants of towns, and workshops were to be at rest on Sunday [*venerabili die Solis*], with an exception in favor of those engaged in agricultural labor." *Encyclopedia Britannica*, Ninth Edition, Volume XXIII, Article "Sunday," page 654.

"Constantine the Great made a law for the whole empire [A.D. 321] that Sunday should be kept as a day of rest in all cities and towns; but he allowed the country people to follow their work." *Encyclopedia Americana,* Article "Sabbath."

"Unquestionably the first law, either ecclesiastical or civil, by which the Sabbatical observance of that day [Sunday] is known to have been ordained, is the edict of Constantine, A.D. 321." *Chambers Encyclopedia*, Article "Sabbath."

Of this edict of Constantine, George Elliott wrote: "To

fully understand the provisions of this legislation, the peculiar position of Constantine must be taken into consideration. He was not himself free from all remains of heathen superstition. It seems certain that before his conversion he had been particularly devoted to the worship of Apollo, the sun-god... The problem before him was to legislate for the new faith in such a manner as not to seem entirely inconsistent with his old practices, and not to come in conflict with the prejudices of his pagan subjects. He names the holy day, not the Lord's day, but the 'day of the sun,' the heathen designation, and thus at once seems to identify it with his former Apollo worship." Reverend George Elliott, *The Abiding Sabbath*, page 229.

However, the Church did not want to be left out, and Eusebius, (bishop during the time of Constantine) wrote of the part the Church had in the change of the Sabbath: "All things whatsoever that it was duty to do on the Sabbath, these we have transferred to the Lord's day [here meaning Sunday]." Eusebius, cited by Robert Cox, *Literature of the Sabbath Question,* Volume 1, page 361.

"Sunday [*dies solis* or 'day of the sun' of the Roman calendar because it was dedicated to the sun], the first day of the week, was adopted by the early Christians as a day of worship... No regulations for its observance are laid down in the New Testament, nor, indeed is its observance even enjoined." Schaff-Herzog, *Encyclopedia of Religious knowledge*, Volume VI, Article Sunday, 3rd Edition, page 2259.

"The first who ever used it [the title Sabbath] to denote the Lord's day [here made to mean Sunday] is one Petrus Alfonsus. He lived about the time that Repurtus did [beginning of the twelfth century], who calls Sunday by the name of Christian Sabbath." Peter Heylyn, *History of the Sabbath*, Part 2, Chapter 2, Section 12.

Chambers' Encyclopedia, to which we can safely trust as being free from any bias in favor of the seventh-day Sabbath, says: "By none of the Fathers before the fourth century is it [Sunday] identified with the Sabbath; nor is the duty of observing it grounded by them either on the fourth commandment or on the precept or example of Jesus or His apostles."

Sir William Domville wrote: "Centuries of the Christian era passed away before the Sunday was observed as a Sabbath. History does not furnish us with a single proof or indication that it was at any time so observed previous to the sabbatical edict of Constantine in A.D. 321." Sir William Domville, *The Sabbath; or an Examination of the Six Texts*, page 291.

THE INFLUENCE OF PAGANISM

After the flood, the first great apostasy against God began with Noah's great grandson, Nimrod. Josephus, the ancient historian, wrote about Nimrod and how he seduced the people of his day to rebel against God: "...it was Nimrod who excited them to such an affront and contempt of God. He was the grandson of Ham, the son of Noah, a bold man, and of great strength of hand... He said he would be revenged on God, if he would have a mind to drown the world again, for that he would build a tower too high for the waters to be able to reach! And that he would avenge himself on God for destroying their forefathers! ...the multitude were very ready to follow the determination of Nimrod, and to esteem it a piece of cowardice to submit to God..." *The Complete Works of Flavius Josephus,* Whiston, 1978, page 30.

Genesis 10:10 says: *"the beginning of his kingdom was Babel."* Nimrod supervised the building of the tower of Babel which became a monument to his rebellion and anger toward God. After God scattered the people from Babel (Genesis 11:8), Nimrod built the city of Nineveh. Emperor worship was common in ancient times, and he was worshipped in Nineveh, as a war-like god, under his deified name, "Ninus." Austen H. Layard, of the British Museum, excavated the ancient city of Nineveh and unearthed over 2500 tablets. These tablets described the ancient history of the Assyrian Empire, and Layard found inscriptions that said it was "Ninus" who built the city. The word "Nineveh" means "The habitation of Ninus."

Assyrian legend says that Nimrod was killed, and his spirit, as a bull, became immortal and flew up to the sun where he became "Beelsamon" or "Lord of the heavens." One still sees Nimrod's influence today in the bull-like constellation named Taurus. After his death, Nimrod's epics as a hunter and warrior were imitated in the Canaanite, Egyptian, Greek, and Roman cultures. The Assyrians, who believed that Nimrod lived in the sun, continued to worship him under the name of "Ninus." The Canaanites worshipped "Beelsamon," or the sun, under the name of "Baal." During the time of Israel in the Old Testament, Baal worship was the greatest rival religion to the worship of God. The Egyptians worshiped the sun as "Osiris," the Romans as "Mars," the Greeks as "Zeus," and the Phoenicians as "Pan." Since Babel was the center of the known world after the flood, and since all civilizations originated there, multitudes of pagan traditions have their origin in the legends of Nimrod.

Babel was the birthplace of sun worship and astrology. From its origin at Babel, traces of this sun worship culture have been found in the history of every nation and society worldwide today. Babylonian astrology had two sacred numbers, the numbers 1 and 7. The number 7 in astrology stood for the seven fate-controlling planets in the zodiac. (Deuteronomy 18 says that astrology is an abomination to God.) The number 1 meant that the sun-worshipper was to give to the heavenly bull-god the first of everything; the first day of the week, the first day of the month, the first day of the year, the first born son, first of the cattle, crops, etc. Of course the sun and Nimrod were only fronts used by Lucifer to get the inhabitants of the earth to worship him instead of the God of heaven.

Gaston H. Halsberghe, in his book, *The Cult of Sol Invictus,* 1972, page 26, says that sun-worship was "one of the oldest components of the Roman religion." A.

Piganiol, in *Histoire de Rome*, 1954, page 229, says that the emperor Augustus (27 B.C.) favored the worship of the sun, and that Anthony, before him, portrayed the sun god on his coins. Halsberghe says that Nero (A.D. 54-68) "honored the sun," and Tacitus tells us that Vespasian (A.D. 69-79) "greeted the rising sun."

By the end of the first century, the veneration of the day of the sun was already a well-rooted tradition in Rome. The first day of the week was dedicated to the heavenly body that came first in importance to pagan worship. Hence the name, "Sunday." Historical records show that Sunday was used as a day of worship ages before the resurrection of Christ. The Romans gave the days of the week their planetary names, and Sunday, was the special holy day for Roman, pagan sun worship. F. Cumont, in his book, *Astrology and Religion Among the Greeks and Romans,* 1912, page 163, wrote: "Sunday, over which the Sun presided, was especially holy." In *The Mysteries of Mithra*, 1956, page 167, we read: "The *dies Solis* [day of the sun] was evidently the most sacred of the week for the faithful of Mithra." Origen, in *Contra Celsum*, Number 6, pages 21,22, says that Celsus (A.D. 140-180) listed the days of the week (using their planetary names) in reverse order enabling Sunday to occupy the significant seventh position.

The fact that Sunday was already established as a day of religious worship in Rome made the step from Sabbath holiness to Sunday holiness a very short one for those early Christians seeking to distance themselves from Judaism. It was especially a short step when one realizes that astrology and sun worship seem to have had such a strong influence on those early Christians. The influence of astrological beliefs on early Christianity can be seen in Jack Lindsay's book, *Origin of Astrology,* 1972, Chapter 20 entitled "Pagans and Christians," pages 373-400. In this chapter Lindsay says that Origen (bishop of the church in Rome) complained that many Christians believed that nothing could happen unless it had been "decreed by the stars." Eusebius (bishop of Caesarea) wrote: "I know many who worship and pray to the Sun." F. A. Regan, in *Dies Dominica*, page 196 wrote; "A suitable, single example of the pagan influence may be had from an investigation of the Christian custom of turning toward the East, the land of the rising sun, while offering their prayers."

The Christian Fathers fought these pagan influences for a time, but then (probably out of frustration) took on an apologetic attitude, adopting many pagan customs into Christianity. This apologetic attitude can be seen in Jerome's *In Die Dominica Paschae Homilia,* where he explains: "If it is called 'day of the Sun' by the pagans, we most willingly acknowledge it as such, since it is on this day that the light of the world has appeared and on this day the Sun [notice the spelling] of Justice has risen." J. A. Jungmann, in *The Early Liturgy to the Time of Gregory the Great*, 1962, page 151, wrote: "Christianity absorbed and made its own what could be salvaged from pagan antiquity, not destroying it but converting it, Christianizing what could be turned to good." A. J. Vermeulen, in *The Semantic Development of Gloria in Early Christian Latin*, 1956, page 170 said: "They [the Church Fathers] took a much easier view of certain pagan customs, conventions, and images and saw no objection, after ridding them of their pagan content, to adapting them to Christian thought."

"We are told in various ways by Eusebius, that Constantine, in order to recommend the new religion to the heathen, transferred into it the outward ornaments to which they had been accustomed in their own." John Henry Cardinal Newman, *An Essay on the Development of Christian Doctrine,* London, 1920, page 373.

The fact that Sunday was already venerated by the Romans made it easy for those early Christians, who were trying to gain favor with Rome, to associate their worship with the symbolism of the pagan sun. Dr. Samuele Bacchiocchi says this was "aimed at gaining from the Emperor a favorable appraisal of Christianity."

It's because of what you have just read that Sunday

has come to be known by many Christians today as "the Lord's day."

THE LORD'S DAY

In chapter one of Revelation, John received a vision of Jesus Christ who instructed him to write what he saw and send it to the seven churches in Asia. In verse 10 he says: *"I was in the Spirit* [or in vision] *on the Lord's day...,"* however he does not tell us which day that was. Many people today speculate that it was Sunday. But remember that no Bible writer ever substantiates this speculation. Our only authority on this matter must be Jesus Himself. Surely He knows which day He is the Lord of. In Mark 2:28 He says: *"Therefore the Son of man is Lord also of the Sabbath."* Here is the only clear, concise statement in all of Scripture as to which day "the Lord's day" is. The Bible Sabbath *is* the Lord's day!

The phrase "the Lord's day" occurs only one time in the entire Bible. When this phrase is used today by Christians it is generally intended to mean Sunday. Sundaykeepers often employ this text in attempted support for the keeping of the first day of the week in place of the seventh-day Bible Sabbath. But is that what John meant by the phrase when he used it? Let's let history set the stage for us so that we can better understand what John meant when he wrote these words.

Because of the persecution of the Jews, Sunday observance began with the Christian church in Rome under bishop Sixtus about A.D. 125 (Eusebius, *Ecclesiastical History*, book 5, chap. 24, par. 14). But prior to Sixtus, in fact as early as the time when John wrote Revelation (A.D. 96), some Christians had begun the practice of annually celebrating the closing days of Christ's life (Eusebius, book 5, chap. 24). Jesus was crucified on Friday at the time of the Jewish Passover. He died just prior to sunset on the fourteenth day of the Jewish month of Nisan. It became a tradition among early Christians to celebrate the crucifixion at the time the Jews celebrated Passover. The Christians took their reckoning date from the Jewish fourteenth day of Nisan. Some Christians celebrated only the day of the crucifixion (always on the fourteenth of Nisan), while others celebrated the three days from the crucifixion to the resurrection. Still others observed the whole time of the Jewish festival (Feast of Unleavened Bread) which lasted until the twenty-first day of Nisan (Eusebius, book 5, chap. 24, par. 2,12,13). In any case the celebration centered around the day of the crucifixion. The fourteenth day of Nisan was observed without concern for which day of the week it fell on, the same way that Christmas is celebrated on December 25 regardless of which day of the week it falls on.

It was this practice that Sixtus undertook to change. About A.D. 125 he changed the emphasis of this yearly celebration from the crucifixion to the resurrection. And he changed the date of the celebration from the fourteenth of Nisan, regardless of the day of the week, to always on Sunday, the first day of the week, in honor of the resurrection. But remember, this was still only an annual celebration and not a weekly one at this time.

Justin Martyr, in his *First Apology*, gives us the *first ever* recorded description of a weekly Sunday observance by Christians about A.D. 155. In this document he referred to the day the Christians observed as "the day of the sun" because he had no other name for it. In other words, Sunday was still not called "the Lord's day" as late as A.D. 155.

In their zeal to establish an early date linking the phrase "Lord's day" with Sunday, the American Tract Society has quoted Justin Martyr as saying: "...on the Lord's day all Christians in the city or country meet together, because that is the day of our Lord's resurrection." (Quoted from *The Bible Dictionary of the American Tract Society*, page 379.) But Justin Martyr never wrote those words, nor did he ever give to Sunday the title of "Lord's day." What follows are his words correctly quoted:

"And on the day called Sunday, all who live in cities or in the country gather together to one place, and the memoirs of the apostles, or the writings of the prophets, are read, as long as time permits..." Justin Martyr, *First Apology*, translated by William Reeves, Section 87, page 127. In the same context he refers to administration of communion at the gathering, with the emblems being also taken by deacons to absent members.

Up through the date of A.D. 155, Sunday was known only as "the day of the sun," or as "the first day of the week." In fact it was not until after A.D. 200 that John's phrase "the Lord's day" began being attached to Sunday.

The first time that Sunday was ever called "the Lord's Day" *in recorded history* was by Clement of Alexandria at the end of the second century A.D. And it was not until the fourth century (A.D. 325), at the Council of Nicaea, that Pope Sylvester imposed the title "Lord's Day" on Sunday. Then in A.D. 364, at the Council of Laodicea, the Catholic hierarchy prescribed Sunday worship and proscribed (condemned) Saturday worship.

Was John referring to Sunday when he wrote the phrase *"the Lord's day"* in Revelation 1:10? I believe not.

The word "Lord's," in Revelation 1:10, is a translation of an adjective used in the Greek phrase *kuriakee heemera*. The adjective *kuriakee* is derived from the regular New Testament word for Lord, *kurios*, with a suffix added to its stem. In English we have no suitable adjective form of "Lord," since the only one we have, "lordly," has come by usage to have a meaning not adaptable to this phrase. The nearest we can come to a proper equivalent is to say "day of the Lord," or as in the text, "Lord's day," meaning a day belonging to the Lord or set apart by the Lord.

Scripture gives us an interesting parallel between "Lord's day" and the phrase "Lord's supper," in 1 Corinthians 11:20. As most all Christians know, this is the supper presided over by Jesus just prior to His crucifixion, and ordained by Him to be observed by His followers *"till He come."* The adjective qualifying "supper" in this verse

45

is the exact same one used to qualify "day" in Revelation 1:10, and it is not used anywhere else in the New Testament. In the case of the "supper," it was instituted by the Lord's setting us the example of how to observe it. In the case of the "day," it was also instituted by the Lord's setting us the example of how to observe it. Scripture sets the Bible Sabbath apart as "the Lord's day." In the Ten Commandments the seventh day is called *"the Sabbath of the Lord thy God"* (Exodus 20:10). In Isaiah, the Lord calls it *"My holy day"* (Isaiah 58:13). In three Gospels, Jesus calls Himself *"Lord of the Sabbath"* (Matthew 12:8; Mark 2:28; Luke 6:5). The seventh-day Sabbath is the only day God ever set apart by resting upon it Himself, and commanding us to *"remember"* to keep it holy. The day was set apart by the Lord's setting us the example of how to observe it. In other words, it is supremely "the Lord's day," as surely as the supper was and is "the Lord's supper."

Clifford Goldstein, in his book, *A Pause For Peace*, 1992, page 95, wrote: "Just because Sunday has been called the Lord's day for years doesn't make it the Lord's day, any more than the fact that people believed for centuries that the earth was the center of the universe makes it so. We shouldn't read *back* into this phrase the meaning of Sunday. Instead, we should use the Bible to read *into* the phrase its *Biblical* meaning, and nothing in Scripture ever calls the first day of the week the Lord's day."

Some Christians teach that John received *new light* in his visions at Patmos, when he wrote Revelation, bidding him to call Sunday by the name of "Lord's day." But a point we need to remember is that John's gospel is dated later than his book of Revelation. John used the phrase "the Lord's day" in A.D. 96 when he wrote Revelation, yet in A.D. 97, when he wrote the Gospel of John, he twice referred to Sunday only as "the first day of the week" (John 20:1,19). Why would John in his gospel call Sunday "the first day of the week," if, in an earlier book, Revelation, he had been instructed to call it "the Lord's day?" John did *not* receive new light in vision at Patmos bidding him to call Sunday "the Lord's day." Rather, I believe that it was consistent for the apostle John to write *kuriakee heemera*, "Lord's day," as a designation for the Sabbath of the Lord.

THE MISSING TEXT

In doing my research for this book, I asked a Sundaykeeping pastor friend of mine for Biblical proof of the change of the Sabbath from the seventh to the first day of the week. While we both agreed that the Bible should be our final authority on any subject, he reluctantly admitted that there is no textual support for Sunday observance. Instead he referred me to the writings of some of the early church fathers such as Ignatius, Barnabas, Justin Martyr, and Clement of Alexandria for his Sunday rational.

Ignatius was Bishop of Antioch at the time of Trajan (A.D. 98-117). He wrote *The Epistle of Ignatius to the Magnesians,* a book which was not included in the authorized New Testament because its content was not believed to be inspired by the Holy Spirit (see *The Lost Books of the Bible*, page 172). And while it's true that in A.D. 101 Ignatius does make a statement favoring the first day instead of the seventh, he also made many other statements renouncing the custom of Sabbath observance. The fact that he urges Christians to stop keeping the Sabbath tells us that the Sabbath was still kept at the turn of the century. Dr. Samuele Bacchiocchi says of Ignatius: "His language suggests that the separation from Judaism was in progress, though the ties had not yet been severed... Ignatius, by urging Christians to differentiate themselves from Jewish practices such as 'sabbatizing,' offers us significant insight on how the existence of anti-Jewish attitudes and efforts contributed to the adoption of Sunday observance." Dr. Samuele Bacchiocchi, *From Sabbath to Sunday,* 1977, pages 213-216.

Ignatius only further reinforces what this book has

been telling you all along. Sunday observance did not begin with Christ or the apostles in Jerusalem, but gradually crept in around the turn of the century as a result of apostasy in the Christian faith.

Barnabas of Alexandria wrote *The Epistle of Barnabas* between A.D. 130 to 138 (see E. Goodspeek, *Apostolic Fathers*, 1950, page 19). While Ignatius makes only an obscure reference to Sunday, Barnabas makes the first explicit reference to the observance of "the day of the sun." His epistle was written as an attack against Judaism, and it reveals how social and theological tensions between Jews and Christians caused the devaluation of the Sabbath and the adoption of a new day of worship by many Christians.

Justin Martyr lived, taught and wrote in Rome under the reign of Antoninus Pius (A.D. 138-161). "He was at first a pagan proponent of Platonism, and subsequently embraced Christianity without abandoning Platonism." (*Encyclopedia Americana,* 1973, Volume 16, page 267.) He is the first contemporary writer to give an extensive description of Sunday worship. Dr. Bacchiocchi writes: "The testimony of Justin, coming from Rome, confirms what we have already gathered from other sources, namely the existence, particularly in the capital city, of deep anti-Judaic feelings... The adoption of a new day of worship appears to have been motivated by the necessity to evidence a clear dissociation from the Jews." (*From Sabbath to Sunday*, pages 233,234.) On page 235 of the same book Dr. Bacchiocchi says: "The diversity of motivations advanced by Justin to justify Sunday worship reflects the effort being made to justify a practice only recently introduced." In other words, at the time of Justin Martyr, Sunday observance had only been "recently introduced" into Christianity as a means of avoiding any semblance of Judaism!

Those Christians who today quote from these sources as proof for the change of the Sabbath must realize that their proof is coming from extra-biblical sources; sources that can hardly be considered theologically correct, as you will see from what you are going to read next.

Clement of Alexandria, born around A.D 150, wrote between A.D. 200 to 215 (see *Encyclopedia Americana*, 1973, Volume 7, page 48). He wrote his 3 epistles, *Protrepticus; Paedagogus;* and *Stromata,* one hundred years after the death of the last apostle. He tells us that by that time the seventh-day Sabbath had "become nothing more than a working day." From his writings we see that the church to which he belonged had gradually ceased to observe the Bible Sabbath, and had begun keeping Sunday in its place as a holy day. But I will leave you to judge just how theologically correct his writings are after you read the following from his works:

"There is a certain bird called Phoenix; of this there is never but one at a time; and that lives 500 years. And when the time of its dissolution draws near, that it must die, it makes itself a nest of frankincense, and myrrh, and other spices into which when its time is fulfilled it enters and dies. But its flesh putrefying, breeds a certain worm, which being nourished with the juice of the dead bird brings forth feathers; and when it is grown to a perfect state, it takes up the nest in which the bones of its parents lie, and carries it from Arabia into Egypt. And flying in open day in the sight of all men, lays it upon the altar of the sun, and so returns from whence it came."

Imagine being compelled to read from such a source as this to prove that "the day of the sun" has taken the place of the Bible Sabbath for the Christian. No wonder the preface to *The Lost Books of the Bible* says these writings were "not included in the authorized New Testament."

Allen Walker wrote: "Since many of the Romans who came into the apostate, or apostatizing, church were sun worshipers before they came in, they were permitted to continue to give certain respect to that day, but were instructed that its observance should have to do with 'the risen Son' rather than 'the rising sun.' Gradually as the pagan element grew in influence and power in the church, the true Sabbath was practically supplanted by Sunday." Allen Walker, *The Law and The Sabbath*, 1953, pages 150,151.

THE SABBATH IN THE NEW TESTAMENT

Over the years, I have heard many Christians reason that the Sabbath is strictly an Old Testament institution. They argue that the Sabbath cannot be found in the New Testament. If you have used this reasoning in the past, maybe it's because you haven't been looking for the Sabbath in the New Testament.

In Matthew 3:15, Jesus, who had no need of baptism, was baptized as our *example*. In John 13:15, Jesus washed the disciples' feet as our *example*. The truth is that Jesus came to this earth to do more than die for our sins. He also came to this earth to live as our *example*. And following His *example*, we are *"to walk, even as He walked."* (1 John 2:6).

Luke 4:16 and Mark 6:2 tell us that Jesus worshipped on the Sabbath day. Matthew 12:8 and Mark 2:28 tell us that Jesus is *"Lord of the Sabbath day."* According to Luke 23:54-24:1, Jesus even honored the Sabbath while in the tomb. But the most convincing proof of the Sabbath in the New Testament comes from Christ's own prophecy in Matthew 24. Jesus, looking some forty years into the future, spoke to His disciples of the destruction of Jerusalem by the Roman general, Titus. Jesus admonished His listeners to watch for certain signs, and then to flee to the mountains. Prophesying this destruction He said in verse 20: *"But pray ye that your flight be not in the winter, neither on the Sabbath day."* This prophecy of Jesus was fulfilled nearly 40 years after He ascended back to heaven when Titus sacked Jerusalem in A.D. 70. Now if Jesus knew that the Sabbath was to be changed to another day after His death, this would have been the perfect opportunity for Him to tell His disciples, whom He was training for evangelism. But He didn't! In fact He told them to pray that they would not have to flee Jerusalem on the Sabbath when they saw His prophecy being fulfilled. Nowhere in Scripture does Jesus even hint at a change in the Bible Sabbath.

Acts 17:2 tells us that it was Paul's *"manner"* (or custom) to worship on the Sabbath day. Acts 13:42 tells us that he also preached to the Gentiles on the Sabbath. If the Christian Sabbath was to be changed to a day other than the Bible Sabbath, here was the perfect opportunity for Paul to explain this change to his Gentile listeners. But he didn't! In fact, nowhere in Scripture does he even hint at a change. Paul clearly taught the Gentiles on the Sabbath in Acts 18:4, and he clearly taught the Jews concerning the Sabbath in Hebrews 4:4-11.

A Bible student can hardly miss finding the Sabbath while reading the New Testament. In fact the Sabbath is given more coverage by the apostles than any other *single* aspect of Christ's ministry. The Gospels (Matthew, Mark, Luke, and John) were not written immediately after Jesus' death, rather they were written between 30 and 60 years after His ascension. The fact that the gospel writers and Paul give so much attention to the Sabbath is indicative of the importance they attached to the Sabbath *at the time of their writing*. These evangelists were writing to encourage their congregations. They were not writing simply a history of what happened, but rather a theological account to promote the Christian faith. Had they believed the Sabbath to be abolished, they would never have encouraged their congregations by even referring to it.

Gerhard Barth, in his book, *Tradition and Interpretation in Matthew*, London, 1963, page 81 says: "In Matthew's congregation the Sabbath was still kept, but not in the same strict sense as in the Rabbinate." If Pastor Matthew and his congregation still kept the Sabbath after Christ's ascension, it is quite evident that Matthew knew nothing of any supposed change of the Sabbath day. A. W. Argyle, in his book, *The Gospel According to Matthew*, Grand Rapids, 1963, page 183, wrote: "The Sabbath was still observed

51

by Christians when Matthew wrote."

The book of Mark was written by John Mark, cousin to Barnabas. Mark was a scribe, who became Peter's interpreter when Peter addressed audiences whose language was other than Aramaic. The book of Mark is believed to be Peter's account of Christ's life, and it was written as a Christian evangelistic tool for non-Jewish readers. The style of writing suggests that it was written in Greek with Latin transliteration so as to be more easily understood by the Romans. What is the significance of this? In Mark 2:27 Jesus said: *"...the Sabbath was made for man, and not man for the Sabbath."* Some 27 years after Christ's ascension, Peter recalled these words of Jesus to teach his Gentile listeners the true meaning of the Sabbath. What was that meaning? That the *"Sabbath was made"* (*ginomai* in the Greek refers to its origin at creation) to insure man's physical and spiritual well-being. *"Not man for the Sabbath"* means that man is not the ultimate arbiter who determines the validity of one of God's commands.

Luke, a physician, and one of Paul's Gentile converts from Antioch authored the book of Luke about A.D. 63 (some 30 years after the ascension), and the book of Acts shortly thereafter. In Luke 1 he introduces us to Christ's earthly parents; in Luke 2 he tells of Christ's birth; in Luke 3 of His baptism; and in chapter 4 he introduces us to Jesus as a habitual Sabbathkeeper. In Luke 4:16 he wrote: *"And He came to Nazareth, where He had been brought up: and, as His **custom** was, He went into the synagogue on the Sabbath day, and stood up for to read."* (emphasis supplied). Luke also refers to Paul as a habitual Sabbathkeeper in Acts 17:2, and wrote of Paul's teaching on the Sabbath in Acts 13:42, Acts 16:13, and Acts 18:4. The word "Sabbath" occurs 21 times in Luke's gospel, and 8 times in the book of Acts. This surely suggests that Luke attached great significance to the day. Luke's intention was to place Jesus before his readers as a model of true Sabbathkeeping.

Luke, being a Gentile, made a habit of pointing out things which were exclusively Jewish. Note the following: *"nation of the Jews"* (Acts 10:22); *"land of the Jews"* (Acts 10:39); *"people of the Jews"* (Acts 12:11); and *"synagogue of the Jews"* (Acts 14:1). And though Luke refers to the Sabbath over and over again, never does he say, "Sabbath of the Jews."

If the Sabbath was not to be kept in the New Testament, someone forgot to tell Matthew, Peter, Paul, Luke and many others who should have known. If *"All Scripture is given by inspiration of God..."* (2 Timothy 3:16), then one must acknowledge that these men wrote what they did under the inspiration of the Holy Spirit, and that neither they, nor any other Bible writer, intended to leave us with the idea that the Sabbath had been changed.

Revelation tells us that God will create this earth new again after the millennium is over. Speaking of this new earth, God, through Isaiah, said: *"...and from one Sabbath to another, shall all flesh come to worship before me, saith the Lord."* (Isaiah 66:23). The Sabbath is not an Old Testament institution, but rather a Bible institution that spans from Eden lost to Eden restored.

"The Sabbath was established originally in no special connection with the Hebrews, but as an institution for all mankind, in commemoration of God's rest after the six days of creation. It was designed for all the descendants of Adam." *Adult Quarterly*, Southern Baptist Convention Series, August 15, 1937.

"The seventh day was blessed and hallowed by God Himself... This commandment is of universal and perpetual obligation... So long, then, as man exists, and the world around him endures, does the law of the early Sabbath remain. It cannot be set aside, so long as its foundations last... It is not the Jewish Sabbath. There is no Jewish element, any more than there is in the third commandment, or the sixth." *Eadie's Biblical Cyclopaedia*, page 561.

THE SABBATH OVER THE CENTURIES

In my research I was able to find many quotations that directly mention the seventh-day Sabbath in every century from the cross to our day. I wish to share just a few of those quotations with you to show that the Bible Sabbath has been kept from the beginning of the Christian era, by both Jew and Gentile alike, and that the early Christians did not consider the Sabbath to be just for the Jews.

The famous historian Josephus (37 to 100 A.D.) wrote while in Rome of the spread of Sabbath observance: "There is not any city of the Grecians, nor any of the barbarians, nor any nation whatsoever, whither our custom of resting on the seventh day hath not come!" Quoted by M'Clatchie, Notes and Queries, Volume 4, Numbers 7, 8, page 100.

Eusebius, writing of those first century Christians who fled from persecution, said: "Then the spiritual seed of Abraham fled to Pella, on the other side of Jordan, where they found a safe place of refuge, and could serve their Master and keep His Sabbath." *Eusebius's Ecclesiastical History*, Book 3, Chapter 5.

First century writer Philo declared the seventh-day Sabbath to be a "festival, not of this or of that city, but of the universe." M'Clatchie, *Notes and Queries*, Volume 4, page 99.

Dr. Morer, writing of the second century Christians, said: "The primitive Christians had a great veneration for the Sabbath, and spent the day in devotion and sermons. And it is not to be doubted but they derived this practice from the Apostles themselves." Dr. T. H. Morer, *Dialogues on the Lord's Day,* London, 1701, page 189.

Mingana, writing of the spread of Christianity during the third century, said, that as early as A.D. 225 there existed large bishoprics of Sabbath-keeping Churches stretching from Palestine to India. Mingana, *Early Spread of Christianity*, Volume 10, page 460.

Professor Edward Brerewood, of Gresham College,

London (Episcopal), says: "The ancient Sabbath did remain and was observed by the Christians of the East Church, above three hundred years after our Saviour's death." Edward Brerewood, *A Learned Treatise of the Sabbath*, page 77.

In fourth century Persia, A.D. 335 to 375 (40 years persecution under Shapur II), the popular complaint against the Christians was that: "They despise our sun-god, they have divine services on Saturday, they desecrate the sacred earth by burying their dead in it." *Truth Triumphant*, page 170.

Historian Lyman Coleman, writing of the fifth century Christians, wrote: "Down even to the fifth century the observance of the Jewish Sabbath was continued in the Christian church." Lyman Coleman, *Ancient Christianity Exemplified*, Chapter 26, Section 2, page 527.

In fifth century Italy, "Ambrose, the celebrated bishop of Milan, said that when he was in Milan he observed Saturday, but when in Rome he observed Sunday. This gave rise to the proverb, 'When you are in Rome, do as Rome does.'" Heylyn, *The History of the Sabbath*, 1612.

The historian Socrates, who wrote about the middle of the fifth century, said: "Almost all the churches throughout the world celebrate the sacred mysteries [communion] on the Sabbath of every week, yet the Christians of Alexandria and at Rome, on account of some ancient tradition, refuse to do this." Socrates Scholasticus, *Ecclesiastical History*, Book 5, Chapter 22, page 404.

W.T. Skene wrote of the sixth century preacher Columba and the Scottish Church: "They seemed to have followed a custom of which we find traces in the early monastic church of Ireland by which they held Saturday to be the Sabbath on which they rested from all their labours." W.T. Skene, *Adamnan Life of St. Columba*, 1874, page 96.

James Moffatt, Professor of Church History at Princeton, writing of the seventh century church in Scotland and Ireland, said: "It seems to have been customary in the Celtic churches of early times, in Ireland as well as

Scotland, to keep Saturday, the Jewish Sabbath, as a day of rest from labour. They obeyed the fourth commandment literally upon the seventh day of the week." James C. Moffatt, D.D., *The Church in Scotland*, page 140.

In A.D. 781 (eighth century China), the famous China Monument was inscribed in marble to tell of the growth of Christianity in China at that time. The inscription, consisting of 763 words, was unearthed in 1625 near the city of Changan and now stands in the "Forest of Tablets," Changan. The following extract from the stone shows that the Sabbath was observed: "On the seventh day we offer sacrifices, after having purified our hearts, and received absolution for our sins. This religion, so perfect and so excellent, is difficult to name, but it enlightens darkness by its brilliant precepts." *Christianity in China*, M. L'Abbe Huc., Volume I, Chapter 2, pages 48,49.

"Bulgaria in the early season of its evangelization (ninth century A.D.) had been taught that no work should be performed on the Sabbath." Hefele, *Conciliengeschicte*, Volume 4, Section 478.

T. Ratcliffe Barnett, in his book on the Catholic Queen Margaret of Scotland, who in 1060 was first to attempt the ruin of Columba's brethren, writes: "In this matter the Scots had perhaps kept up the traditional usage of the ancient Irish Church which observed Saturday instead of Sunday as the day of rest." Barnett, *Margaret of Scotland: Queen and Saint*, page 97.

"The observance of Saturday is, as everyone knows, the subject of a bitter dispute between the Greeks and the Latins." Neale, *A History of the Holy Eastern Church*, Volume 1, page 731.

"The Sabbath was observed by the Celtic church as late as the eleventh century." Andrew Lange, *A History of Scotland*, 1909, Volume 1, page 96.

"Traces of Sabbath-keepers are found in the times of Gregory I, Gregory VII, and in the twelfth century in Lombardy." *Strong's Cyclopedia*, Volume 1, page 660.

"Erasmus testifies that even as late as about 1500 the

Bohemians not only kept the seventh day scrupulously, but also were called Sabbatarians." Cox, *The Literature of the Sabbath Question*, Volume 2, pages 201,202.

About the year 1520 many of the Sabbath-keepers in Europe found shelter on the estate of Lord Leonhardt of Lichtenstein, "as the princes of Lichtenstein held to the observance of the true Sabbath." J.N. Andrews, *History of the Sabbath*, page 649.

(Switzerland, 1592) "The observance of the Sabbath is a part of the moral law. It has been kept holy since the beginning of the world." Quoted from the noted Swiss writer, R. Hospinian, 1592.

(Lichtenstein, 1599) "The Sabbatarians teach that the outward Sabbath, i.e. Saturday, still must be observed. They say that Sunday is the Pope's invention." *Refutation of the Sabbath,* by Wolfgang Capito.

(England, 1668) "Here in England are about nine or ten churches that keep the Sabbath, besides many scattered disciples, who have been eminently preserved." Stennet's letters of 1668 and 1670, Cox, *The Literature of the Sabbath Question,* Volume 1, page 268.

"We can trace these opinions over the whole extent of Sweden of that day, from Finland and northern Sweden. In the district of Upsala the farmers kept Saturday in place of Sunday. About the year 1625 this religious tendency became so pronounced in these countries that not only large numbers of the common people began to keep Saturday as the rest day, but even many priests did the same." *History of the Swedish Church*, Volume 1, page 256.

"We will now endeavour to show that the sanctification of the Sabbath has its foundation and its origin in a law which God at creation itself established for the whole world, and as a consequence thereof is binding on all men in all ages." *Evangelisten*, Stockholm, May 30, 1863, page 169.

There are countless other quotations which I have not included for the sake of space. With all the evidence available today, it is easy to see that Sunday observance did not originate with Christ, the apostles, or that early primitive Christian community in Jerusalem.

IS TODAY'S CHRISTIAN BOUND BY GOD'S LAW?

Some people might say, **But the above discussion isn't really necessary, because today's Christian is no longer bound by God's Law**. To those good people who believe we are no longer bound by the Ten Commandment Law, thank you for being so patient.

If you are one of the many people who believe that all or part of the Ten Commandments have been abolished, you are not alone. This is a popular misconception today. Here are some of the Bible texts that people use to support this belief:

> **Romans 6:14**: *"...for ye are not under the law, but under grace."*
> **Romans 10:4**: *"For Christ is the end of the law for righteousness to every one that believeth."*
> **Galatians 3:13**: *"Christ hath redeemed us from the curse of the law..."*
> **Colossians 2:16**: *"Let no man therefore judge you in meat, or in drink, or in respect of an holyday, or of the new moon, or of the sabbath days."*

I want to address each one of these questions individually, but first let's lay a good foundation so that our understanding can be more complete.

If you believe that a law was abolished, or nailed to the cross, you're right! Surprised? Yes, you're right! But the question is, which law? For you see, two laws were given (or put into written form) on mount Sinai, but only one of them was abolished when Christ died on the cross. Let me explain what I mean.

58

Exodus 24:12 says: *"And the Lord said unto Moses, Come up to me into the mount, and be there: and I will give thee tables of stone, and a law, and commandments which I have written; that thou mayest teach them."* Exodus 31:18 says: *"And He gave unto Moses, when He had made an end of communing with him upon mount Sinai, two tables of testimony, tables of stone, written with the finger of God."* These texts refer to God's Moral Law, the Ten Commandments. This we will call law number one.

Now there was another law besides the Ten Commandments that God gave to Israel on mount Sinai. But this one He did not speak directly to the people, nor did He write this law on tables of stone. God dictated this second law to Moses while Moses wrote it in a book. Turn with me to Deuteronomy 31:9 where we read: *"And Moses wrote this law, and delivered it unto the priests the sons of Levi, which bare the ark of the covenant of the Lord, and unto all the elders of Israel."* Verses 24-26 say: *"And it came to pass, when Moses had made an end of writing the words of this law in a book, until they were finished, that Moses commanded the Levites, which bare the ark of the covenant of the Lord, saying, Take this book of the law, and put it in the side of the ark of the covenant of the Lord your God, that it may be there for a witness against thee."* This is law number two.

God wrote the Moral Law of the Ten Commandments on stone with His finger. Moses wrote the Ceremonial Law in a book. We know what the Moral Law is. What was the Ceremonial Law?

If we could liken the Moral Law to the Constitution of the United States, then we could liken the Ceremonial Law to an amendment to the Constitution. An amendment is something that enables us to live up to the Constitution. God gave the Ceremonial Law to Moses to enable the Israelites (spiritually illiterate after 400 years in Egypt) to live up to His Moral Law, the Ten Commandments. The Ceremonial Law was a drama of the plan of salvation in miniature. It was given as a teaching device. It was given to help those uneducated, brutalized people understand the plan of salvation, and that breaking the Moral Law by sinning would some day cause the Saviour to give His life as a sacrifice for their sins. All the blood that was shed in this sacrificial, ceremonial system represented Christ's blood that would be shed to redeem all sinners one day. I encourage you to spend some time and look up the following texts on these two laws, the Moral and the Ceremonial, so that you will have it clear in your own mind.

MORAL LAW (Ten Commandments)
Exodus 24:12 .... Written by God
Exodus 31:18 .... Written on stone
Deuteronomy 10:5 .... Placed inside of ark
Psalms 19:7 .... Law is perfect
Psalms 111:7,8 .... Law is eternal
James 2:10-12 .... Law of Liberty

CEREMONIAL LAW (Law of Moses)
Deuteronomy 31:9. .... Written by Moses
Deuteronomy 31:24 .... Written in a book
Deuteronomy 31:26 .... Placed on side of ark
Hebrews 7:19 .... Made nothing perfect
Ephesians 2:15 .... Abolished by Christ

Many people today, while familiar with the Ten Commandment Law, have never heard of the Law of Moses (known as the Ceremonial Law) before. But the fact is that Jesus Himself made reference to the Law of Moses in John 7:23 when He said to the Pharisees: *"If a man on the Sabbath day receive circumcision, that the law of Moses should not be broken; are ye angry at Me, because I have made a man every whit whole on the Sabbath day?"* The following statements will also help you to see the distinction between the Moral and the Ceremonial Laws:

Reverend Charles Buck, writing in *A Theological Dictionary* under the article "Law," page 230 says: "Ceremonial Law is that which prescribes the rite of worship used under the Old Testament. These rites were typical of Christ [meaning the sacrifices typified Christ's sacrifice for sinners], and were obligatory only till Christ had finished His work, and began to erect His gospel church."

In *The Constitution Of The Presbyterian Church In The United States Of America*, Chapter 19, par. 3, you will find the statement: "Beside the law, commonly called moral, God was pleased to give to the people of Israel, as a church under age, ceremonial laws, containing several typical ordinances, partly of worship, prefiguring Christ, His grace, actions, sufferings, and benefits; and partly holding forth diverse instructions of moral duties. All which ceremonial laws are now abrogated under the New Testament."

John Wesley, in *Sermons On Several Occasions,* Volume 1, pages 221, 222 wrote: "This handwriting of ordinances our Lord did blot out, take away, and nail to His cross [Colossians 2:14]. But the Moral Law contained in the Ten Commandments, and enforced by the prophets, He did not take away... The Moral Law stands on an entirely different foundation from the ceremonial or ritual law... Every part of this law [Ten Commandments] must remain in force upon all mankind and in all ages."

In *The Thirty-nine Articles of Religion of the Church of England*, Article VII reads: "Although the law given from God by Moses, as touching ceremonies and rites, do not bind Christian men, nor the civil precepts thereof ought of necessity to be received in any commonwealth; yet notwithstanding, no Christian man whatsoever is free from the obedience of the commandments which are called moral."

Article VI of *The American Revision by the Protestant Episcopal Church* reads exactly the same as the above statement by the Church of England, and makes the same distinction between the Moral and the Ceremonial laws.

Article VI of *The Doctrines and Discipline of the Methodist Episcopal Church* reads the same and makes the exact same distinction between the Moral and Ceremonial laws.

The Irish Articles of Religion carry a close variation of the same statement. Article 84 states: "Although the law given from God by Moses as touching ceremonies and rites be abolished...yet, notwithstanding, no Christian man whatsoever is freed from the obedience of the commandments which are called moral."

The Westminister Confession of Faith, Chapter XX, Article I, states: "...under the New Testament the liberty of Christians is further enlarged in their freedom from the yoke of the ceremonial law, to which the Jewish Church was subjected."

The Sunday School Times, July 23, 1932 makes the following declaration on the Ten Commandment Law: "To know God is to love God. The commandments were given that men might know Jehovah God, the God of love and the God of holiness. To love God is to obey Him. God's law is an expression of God's love... To have faith in the God of mercy and love is to have the righteousness of Abraham, and of Moses, and the heart of love to God to keep these commandments, by His grace."

Now notice the April 21, 1934 edition of the same *Sunday School Times* with reference to the Ceremonial Law: "Christ fulfilled and thereby canceled forever every jot and tittle of the Ceremonial Law... Paul's argument against 'the law' was aimed at this rabbinical code; and at the continuance of the Ceremonial Law which Christ's redemptive work had canceled."

The Ceremonial Law did exist, and it was this law of ordinances (sacrifices, circumcision, ritual feasts, etc.) that was abolished at the cross, not the *Ten Commandments.* Every aspect of the Ceremonial Law pointed to, or typified Christ as the Lamb of God who would take away the sins of the world. Ephesians 2:15 says: *"Having abolished in His flesh the enmity, even the law of commandments contained in ordinances..."* Hebrews chapter 10 tells us that after Christ died on the cross there was to be no more sacrifice for sin (verse 26), because Christ died *"once for all"* (verse 10) for our sins. The Ceremonial Law is the only law that made provision for animal sacrifices. The animal sacrifice provided a way for man to express his belief that someday God would send the Lamb of God to die as his substitute. Those sacrifices represented, or pointed forward to Christ's ultimate sacrifice for us on the cross. Therefore it was this law that commanded those sacrifices that was abolished when Christ died on the cross.

The day before Jesus died, a man conscious of sin was under obligation to sacrifice an animal as an expression of his faith that God would send His Son to die as his substitute. But the next day after Jesus died, it was no longer proper to kill an animal, because to do so would be to deny Jesus had died. Since Jesus' death we no longer bring a sacrifice. We can see that this regulation came to an end at the cross, but it was not a part of the Moral Law.

The point is, the Ten Commandment Law was meant by God to last forever. That's why He wrote it on stone. Psalms 111:7,8 says: *"The works of His hands are verity and judgment; all His commandments are sure. They stand fast for ever and ever, and are done in truth and upright-ness."* But the Ceremonial Law was meant to last only until the Lamb of God could give His life as a sacrifice for us all. Today we look back at the cross. We do not need the sacrificial system anymore. But the Children of Israel had to look forward to the cross. The Ceremonial Law (like a constitutional amendment) was given to *help them* look forward to Christ's death. Once Christ had died, people no longer had to be pointed forward to His death. Prior to the cross, Christ was showing His people through types and symbols just how salvation works. But after the cross, those types and symbols were no longer needed, because Christ became the reality.

Paul occasionally makes reference to the "law" as being abolished. Yet in Romans 3:31 he says: *"Do we then make void the law through faith? God forbid: yea, we establish the law."* Is Paul contradicting himself? Not at all. He understood the difference between the Moral Law and the Ceremonial Law. When he referred to the "law" as being abolished, he assumed that his readers would also understand that difference. The context is generally sufficient to make clear which law Paul intended. Remember what we read earlier? "Paul's argument against 'the law' was aimed at this rabbinical code; and at the continuance of the Ceremonial Law which Christ's redemptive work had canceled." (Quoted above in *The Sunday School Times.*) When Paul referred to the "abolished law" he was referring to the Ceremonial Law of Moses that commanded circumcision and sacrifices, not to the Moral Law of God. Those today who hold that Paul spoke and wrote against the Ten Commandment Law put Paul at odds with Christ. Paul indeed ignored the Ceremonial Law and taught that circumcision was without value, but when it came to the Moral Law, he stood exactly where Christ stood.

Many Christians today try to argue against the existence of these two laws. But to lump all law into one, and to say it is now abolished, is to say that the Bible presents a hopeless series of contradictions. That there are two laws, only one of which was abolished, will be plain from the reading of the following texts:

> *"Having abolished in His flesh the enmity, even the law of commandments contained in ordinances."* (Ephesians 2:15)
> *"For the priesthood being changed, there is made of necessity a change also of the law."* (Hebrews 7:12)
> *"Blotting out the handwriting of ordinances that was against us, which was contrary to us, and took it out of the way, nailing it to His cross."* (Colossians 2:14)

The Bible is clear that in addition to this abolished law was another law that was not abolished. The following texts prove this beyond all controversy:

> *"And it is easier for heaven and earth to pass, than one tittle of the law to fail."* (Luke 16:17)
>
> *"Do we then make void the law through faith? God forbid: yea we establish the law."* (Romans 3:31)
>
> *"For whosoever shall keep the whole law, and yet offend in one point, he is guilty of all."* (James 2:10)

If we try to lump all law into one, and do not acknowledge the existence of both laws, we make the first three of these verses contradict the other three.

Billy Graham wrote: "The word 'Law' is used by the New Testament writers in two senses. Sometimes it refers to the Ceremonial Law of the Old Testament, which is concerned about ritual matters and regulations... From this law Christians are indeed free. But the New Testament also speaks of the Moral Law, which is of a permanent, unchanging character and is summarized in the Ten Commandments." Associated Press Dispatch, *Chicago Tribune.*

"We believe that the Law of God [Ten Commandments] is the eternal and unchangeable rule of His moral government." *Baptist Church Manual*, Article 12.

"The commandments of God given to Moses in the mount Horeb are as binding today as ever they have been since the time when they were proclaimed in the hearing of the people." Dwight L. Moody, *Weighed and Wanting,* page 15.

"By disowning the Law [Ten Commandments], men utterly subvert the gospel." *Baptist Publication Society*, Tract 64, pages 2-6.

"We hear a lot about ethics and morality. We like to think that we're sophisticated and refined as sinners, but we're not. Sin has not changed. The Ten Commandments are still God's standard... God never changes. The Moral Law is absolute forever..." Dr. Billy Graham, *Decision,* April 1989.

"I wonder exceedingly how it came to be imputed to

me that I should reject the Law of Ten Commandments...
Whosoever abrogates the Law must of necessity abrogate
sin also." Martin Luther, *Spiritual Antichrist*, pages 71,72.

"For up to this day mankind has absolutely trifled with
the original and most specific revelation of the holy God,
the ten words written upon the tables of the Law from
Sinai." *Crown Theological Library*, page 178. (Lutheran)

"No Christian whatsoever is free from the obedience
of the commandments which are called moral." *Methodist
Church Discipline*, 1904, page 23.

"We must not imagine that the coming of Christ has
freed us from the authority of the Law [Ten Command-
ments]; for it is the eternal rule of a devout and holy life,
and must therefore be as unchangeable as the justice of
God, which it embraced, is constant and uniform." John
Calvin, *Commentary On A History Of The Gospels*, Volume 1, page 277. (Presbyterian)

"The law of Ten Commandments has to do with moral
principles, and these are unchanging in any dispensation."
The Sunday School Times, October 17, 1948.

"The Law of God must be perpetual. There is no
abrogation of it, nor amendment of it. It is not to be toned
down or adjusted to our fallen condition; but every one of
the Lord's righteous judgments abideth for ever." Charles
H. Spurgeon, *Spurgeon's Expository Encyclopedia,* by
Baker.

ORIGIN OF THE NO-LAW TEACHING

The idea that the Ten Commandments were abolished
at the cross is echoed and reechoed today from many
directions. But it has not always been this way. In fact, this
no-law belief has only been taught for a little more than
a hundred years.

Nowhere in the Bible or in the writings of the reformers do we find any support for the idea that a person who
is justified can remain unsanctified. That is a topic about
which the reformers had much to say. Martin Luther,

whose discovery of the Biblical truth about justification by faith launched the Reformation, wrote: "For just as natural as it is for the tree to produce fruit, so natural is it for faith to produce good works... Not that man should become good by works, but that man should thereby prove and see the difference between false and true faith. For wherever faith is right it does good. If it does no good, it is then certainly a dream and a false idea of faith." Martin Luther, *Justification by Faith,* quoted by Warren Wiersbe, *Classic Sermons of Faith and Doubt,* 1985, page 78.

John Calvin, who vigorously defended the doctrine of justification by faith, wrote: "We acknowledge that faith and works are necessarily connected." John Calvin, *Institutes of the Christian Religion,* 3:16:1. John Olin quoted Calvin on another occasion as saying: "If you would duly understand how inseparable faith and works are, look to Christ...and wherever Christ is not, there is no righteousness, nay, there is no faith; for faith cannot apprehend Christ for righteousness without the Spirit of sanctification." John C. Olin, *A Reformation Debate,* 1966, page 68.

The Puritans and early English Reformers all believed and taught righteousness by faith. They believed in salvation by faith alone in Jesus Christ (justification), but that that faith experience must be followed by obedience (sanctification). Ryle, Spurgeon, White, Moody, Hodge, Warfield, Machen, and Jonathan Edwards all rejected the notion that justification and sanctification could be disjoined or separated, and that sanctification might be considered optional.

The Bible teaches that believers are saved and fully justified by faith alone, before their faith ever produces a single righteous work (Ephesians 2:8). It teaches that faith inevitably produces a changed life (2 Corinthians 5:17); that repentance is a change of heart, which produces a change of behavior (Luke 3:8; Acts 26:18-20); that true repentance is a turning from sin (1 John 2:1-6; Acts 3:19; Luke 24:47); that those who truly love Jesus will long to obey Him (John 14:15,23); that obedience is evidence that one's faith is real (1 John 2:3); and that those who remain unwilling to obey are not truly converted (1 John 2:4).

Obedience to the Law of God is at the very heart of the gospel message. So where did this no-law teaching that we hear so much about today come from? It originated with a form of Bible interpretation called Dispensationalism. John Nelson Darby is considered by most authorities as the father of modern Dispensationalism. Darby was born in London on November 18, 1800. He enrolled in Trinity College in Dublin, Ireland in 1815, graduating four years later in 1819. He was ordained an Anglican priest in 1826, and pastored for one year in County Wicklow, south of Dublin. But in 1827 he had an accident that would change his life (and the face of Christianity) forever. He was thrown from a horse against a doorpost, and during his lengthy convalescence, he began formulating ideas on something that would later come to be known as Dispensationalism.

Dispensationalism was Darby's method of explaining what he viewed as contradictions in the Bible. It revolves entirely around the nation of Israel, and demands a literal fulfillment of prophecy to literal Israel. In other words, it rejects Jesus' statement in Matthew 21:43 that says that because Israel rejected the Son of God, they would be rejected by God. And it rejects Paul's statement in Galatians 3:26-29 that says that anyone who now accepts Christ is counted as *"Abraham's seed,"* becoming spiritual Israel. Galatians 3:29 says: *"And if ye be Christ's, then are ye Abraham's seed, and heirs according to the promise."* This means that anyone who now accepts Jesus as their Saviour becomes an heir to the promises that were once given to Abraham's literal seed, Israel. To reject the belief that all true Christians today, regardless of nationality, are spiritual Israel, is to leave oneself no alternative but to embrace Darby's Dispensationalism. The primary difference between covenant theology and dispensational theology is that Dispensationalism rejects the teaching that the church is now spiritual Israel. This difference causes many other compounded problems which have led to the no-law teaching that we see today.

Darby's views on Dispensationalism were brought to the United States in 1909 by Cyrus I. Scofield. Scofield, who authored *The Scofield Reference Bible,* included a note in his reference Bible that contrasted "legal obedience" as the condition of salvation in the Old Testament, and "acceptance of Christ" as the condition of salvation in the New Testament (see *The Scofield Reference Bible*, New York, 1917, page 1115). Clarence Larkin popularized Scofield's teachings with his dispensational charts that were first published in 1918, and can still be found in circulation to this day. Lewis Sperry Chafer, one of Scofield's students, wrote Dispensationalism's first unabridged *Systematic Theology*, that has become the standard for the seminary he co-founded, Dallas Theological Seminary. A most recent graduate of Dallas Theological Seminary is Hal Lindsey who popularized dispensational theology in his book *The Late Great Planet Earth.*

Scofield, Larkin, and Chafer pitted justification against sanctification, faith against obedience, and grace against the law. Through their writings, charts, and elaborate footnotes, they were able to isolate salvation from repentance, and faith from works. They believed that law and grace could not coexist side by side, and therefore followed Darby's lead in dividing Biblical time into segments (or dispensations) where one or the other (law or grace) existed exclusively by itself. Chafer, in his book, *Systematic Theology*, ended up with an "age of law" that was pure legalism, and an "age of grace" that was pure antinomianism. Antinomianism is the belief that Christians are no longer bound by God's Moral Law. It makes sanctification, or obedience to God, optional. This antinomian influence is widespread today and can be seen in the writings of such men as Zane Hodges, who wrote in his book, *Absolutely Free!*, that repentance is not essential to the gospel message (pages 44-46), and that submission to God is not in any sense a condition for eternal life (page 172). Another author promoting antinomianism is Charles Ryrie, who wrote in his book, *So Great Salvation*, that no turning from sin is required for salvation (page 99), and that neither dedication nor willingness to be dedicated to Christ are issues in salvation (page 74).

When one throws God's law out the window, there remains no Biblical standard for righteousness. Without God's standard each individual is left to set his own standard, and from this has evolved the premise that Jesus came to save us in our sins, not from our sins.

Writing about the effect Dispensationalism has had on Christianity, Jeffrey Wilson wrote: "Today's 'Christianity' is in a state of disarray and decay, and the condition is deteriorating year by year. The truth of God's Word has been watered down and compromised to reach a common denominator that will appeal to and accommodate the largest number of participants. The result is a hybrid Christianity which is essentially man-centered, materialistic and worldly, and shamefully dishonouring to the Lord Jesus Christ. This shameful degeneracy is due in large part to the erroneous gospel that is presented by many today around the world." Jeffrey E. Wilson, *The Authentic Gospel*, 1990, page 1.

DOES THE CHRISTIAN HAVE TO KEEP THE LAW OF GOD?

Some people have the idea today that they do not have to keep God's Law because of **Romans 6:14**. Let's read it together: *"For sin shall not have dominion over you: for ye are not under the law, but under grace."* Is this text telling us that we no longer have to keep the Ten Commandments? Not at all. Let me explain. 1 John 3:4 tells us: *"sin is the transgression of the law,"* and Romans 5:13 tells us: *"sin is not imputed* [attributed] *when there is no law."* In other words, if there was no Law there could be no sin. Romans 3:20 says: *"Therefore by the deeds of the law there shall no flesh be justified in His sight: for by the* *law is the knowledge of sin."*

Without speed limits on our highways there could be no such thing as speeding. Likewise, without the Ten Commandment Law there could be no such thing as sin. The Law does not save us. That would be legalism. The Law only shows us what sin is. Just as a mirror shows us that our faces are dirty (James 1:22-25), the Law shows us the dirt of sin. And just as the mirror cannot clean our faces once it has revealed the dirt, the Law cannot save us once it has revealed the sin. The *only* purpose of the Law is to point out sin. Paul understood this principle perfectly. That's why he wrote in Romans 3:31: *"Do we then make void the law through faith? God forbid: yea, we establish the law."* This same thought is carried forward in Romans 7:7: *"What shall we say then? Is the law sin? God forbid. Nay, I had not known sin, but by the law: for I had not known lust, except the law had said, Thou shalt not covet."* Without the Law there would be nothing to point out what sin is.

So then how are we saved? Ephesians 2:8 tells us: *"For by grace are ye saved through faith; and that not of yourselves: it is the gift of God."* **What is grace**? Grace comes from the Greek *charis*, and it means "a manifestation of favor; mercy; clemency; pardon; immunity." Charles Hodges, professor of systematic theology at Princeton said: "Grace means a favourable disposition, or kind feeling toward the dependent, or unworthy." The distinctive meaning attached to the term "grace" in the New Testament is that of the abundant, saving love of God toward sinners as revealed in Jesus Christ. It is God's unlimited, all-inclusive, transforming love toward sinful man. Grace is not merely God's mercy and willingness to forgive, but it is His active, energizing, transforming power to save lost humanity. It is the wonderful divine mercy and undeserved favor that flows from the great loving heart of God.

Salvation is not now, and never has been, by works of the law. Salvation comes only through faith in the saving grace of Jesus Christ. There is nothing that any one of us can possibly *do* to earn salvation. And because of this there is a regrettable misunderstanding about the relationship between law and grace today.

If you were to call together a representative group of evangelical believers today, and ask them the question, "Is law opposed to grace?", the answer in most cases would be "Yes." This is because no theological drum is more soundly thumped today than the belief of "law *verses* grace." Law and grace are thus pitted against one another. But it is only in the mind of the person who has made law a means of salvation that this is a problem. The law is designed to reveal sin; grace is designed to save from sin. No conflict can possibly exist between these two. Each serves its specific function in the plan of God, and if understood properly, neither trespasses on the function of the other.

So I ask you, "grace" is a pardon from what?—clemency from what?—immunity from what?—From the wages of sin! Romans 6:23 says: *"For the wages of sin is death..."* Again, **what is sin**? 1 John 3:4 tells us: *"Whosoever committeth sin transgresseth also the law: for sin is the transgression of the law."* The law points out our sin and that is all it does. The law condemns us to death as sinners, but once we see our sins, and with humble heart confess them to Jesus, by His grace He pardons us from the condemnation of the law. That's why Paul said in Romans 8:1: *"There is therefore now no condemnation to them which are in Christ Jesus..."* I believe the following story will help you to understand how law and grace must work together:

When a Man Cannot Be Pardoned

God is gracious, but he will not force the acceptance of His grace upon men. In 1829 George Wilson, in Pennsylvania, was sentenced to be hanged by a United States Court for robbing the mail and for murder. President Andrew Jackson pardoned him, but this was refused, and Wilson insisted that it was not a pardon unless he accepted it. That was a point of law never before raised, and the President called the Supreme Court to decide. Chief Justice John Marshall gave the following decision: "A pardon is a paper, the value of which depends upon its acceptance by the person implicated. It is hardly to be supposed that one under sentence of death would refuse to accept a pardon, but if it is refused, it is no pardon. George Wilson must be hanged!" And he was hanged. Provisionally the Gospel of Christ which is the power of God unto salvation is for everyone irrespective of what he may be or what he may have done. Practically, it is only to "every one that believeth."

  —*Sunday School Times*

If we do not accept the pardon granted to us by Jesus, then the condemnation of the law must remain. The pardon (grace) must be accepted by the sinner. If he refuses to accept it, he is still condemned by the law.

There is a distinction between being under the *jurisdiction* of the law, and being under the *condemnation* of the law. All of humanity is under the jurisdiction of God's law, the same as all citizens of the United States are under the jurisdiction of the laws of this country. When a person breaks the laws of the United States, he then falls under the condemnation of the laws of this country. Grace operates to free the repentant sinner from the *condemnation* of God's law, not from the *jurisdiction* of God's law. "Antinomianism" is a term used for the belief that all or part of the Moral Law has been abolished by grace. Yet if one could be removed from the jurisdiction of God's law, then sin would cease to exist, there would be no further need for grace, and henceforth, no further need of a Saviour.

This makes **Romans 6:14** a little easier to understand. Let's read it together again: *"For sin shall not have dominion over you: for ye are not under the law* [meaning its condemnation]*, but under grace* [pardon from the penalty of the Law]*."* 1 Timothy 1:9 makes this very clear:

73

"Knowing this, that the law is not made for a righteous man, but for the lawless and disobedient..." The law is still there to condemn those who choose to disobey, while the righteous man is pardoned by the wonderful grace of God. Therefore the law can no longer condemn the righteous man because he is now forgiven under grace. G. Campbell Morgan wrote: "It is only when grace enables men to keep the law, that they are free from it; just as a moral man who lives according to the laws of the country is free from arrest." Morgan, *The Ten Commandments,* 1901, page 23. Law and grace must work hand in hand. After all, if the Ten Commandment Law had been abolished, there would be nothing to point out what sin is, and there would be nothing standing between the sinner who refuses to accept Jesus, and the sinner who accepts Jesus and is pardoned from his sins. They would both ultimately receive the same reward.

The second text that I hear people use in defense of an abolished law is **Romans 10:4**: *"For Christ is the end of the law for righteousness to every one that believeth."* Does this mean that the Ten Commandment Law ended with the death of Christ? No, it does not. The Greek word for "end" in this verse is *telos.* It can be translated "goal" or "objective." We also find this same Greek word *telos* in James 5:11: *"Behold, we count them happy which endure. Ye have heard of the patience of Job, and have seen the end of the Lord..."* Now we all know that the Lord did not come to an end! This means the "goal" or "objective" of the Lord. We often hear someone say that they are working toward a certain end. This means they are striving to reach a certain goal, and that is what Paul is saying in Romans 10:4: *"For Christ is the end* [goal or objective] *of the law for righteousness to every one that believeth."* The Lord did not come to an end in James 5:11, and the law did not come to an end in Romans 10:4. Remember what Jesus said in Matthew 5:18? *"**Till heaven and earth pass,** one jot or one tittle shall in no wise pass from the law, till all be fulfilled."* (emphasis supplied).

74

This brings up another question. Many people believe that the word "fulfil" here in Matthew 5:17,18 means "to do away with" or "to destroy." Let's read the text again. Jesus said: *"Think not that I am come to destroy the law, or the prophets: I am not come to destroy, but to fulfil."* If the word "fulfil" means "to do away with" or "to destroy" the text hardly makes any sense. It would read something like this, "Think not that I am come to destroy the law, or the prophets: I am not come to destroy, but to do away with or destroy." Do you see how silly that sounds? Actually the word "fulfil" comes from the Greek *pleroo* which means "to accomplish" or "to put into effect." We find *pleroo* also used in Matthew 3:15: *"And Jesus answering said unto him, Suffer it to be so now: for thus it becometh us to fulfil all righteousness."* Was Jesus saying, "It becometh us to do away with all righteousness?" Not at all. In reality Jesus was saying: *"Think not that I am come to destroy the law, or the prophets: I am not come to destroy, but to fulfil* [accomplish or put into effect]. *For verily I say unto you, Till heaven and earth pass* [at His second coming], *one jot or one tittle shall in no wise pass from the law, till all be fulfilled* [accomplished or put into effect]." We do not cancel traffic laws by fulfilling them, but rather we validate them. We do not cancel a contract by fulfilling it, rather we validate it. Jesus knew that someone would misunderstand His words here in Matthew 5:17. That's why He began the verse with: *"Think not that I am come to destroy the law..."*

Unfortunately, I feel that too many people today are trying to make the Bible say what *they* want it to say. I believe that this is often an attempt to make a case for not keeping all of God's commandments, especially the seventh-day Sabbath. No one ever seems to have a problem with the other nine commandments. Do not try to make the Bible fit the theology of your life, rather, try to bring your life into line with the theology of the Bible.

What about the book of Galatians? Does Galatians release us from keeping the law? Again it depends on which law you are referring to. If you are referring to the Moral Law, the answer is no. If you are referring to the Ceremonial Law, the answer is yes. Remember what we read earlier: "Paul's argument against 'the law' was aimed at this rabbinical code; and at the continuance of the Ceremonial Law which Christ's redemptive work had canceled." (Quoted in *The Sunday School Times*, April 21, 1934.) Try reading Galatians again with this in mind and I believe you will come away with an entirely new understanding.

The entire theme of Galatians has to do with whether or not the new Gentile converts were bound to keep the old Jewish ordinances such as circumcision or not. Had the Jewish converts to Christianity not been so steeped in the traditions of their forefathers, had they completely understood that those ceremonies which pointed people forward to Jesus' death on the cross were to end at the cross, they would not have followed Paul around trying to force the Gentile converts to observe the Ceremonial Law. But the fact is that they did not understand, just as many Christians today do not understand about the Ten Commandments. Those who teach that we no longer have to honor the Ten Commandments are making the same mistake in reverse that the Judaizers made with the Galatian Christians.

Acts 15:1 illustrates the struggle Paul had with the Judaizers at Galatia: *"And certain men which came down from Judaea taught the brethren* [Gentile converts], *and said, Except ye be circumcised after the manner of Moses, ye cannot be saved."* They were trying to force the new Gentile converts to comply with the Ceremonial Law of circumcision. This shows that they did not understand that the sacrifices, ceremonies, and ordinances that pointed forward to Christ's death were to end when Christ died on the cross.

Paul and Barnabas and these Judaizers had a *"dissension and disputation"* about this (Acts 15:2), and they determined to go to Jerusalem to the Church headquarters to resolve the disagreement. In verses 4 and 5 we read: *"And when they were come to Jerusalem, they were received of the church, and of the apostles and elders, and they declared all things that God had done with them. But there rose up certain of the sect of the Pharisees which believed* [these were Pharisees who believed in Christ], *saying, That it was needful to circumcise them, and to command them to keep the law of Moses."* Though these Pharisees were converted to Christianity, they tried to bring all the Jewish rites and rituals into their new faith. The matter ended when James, the Lord's brother, pointed out that new converts to Christianity did not have to follow these old covenant ceremonial ordinances and laws (verse 19).

Paul believed in salvation by faith alone in the blood of Jesus Christ. In Galatians 3 he tells us that the observance of a law, any law, will never save a person. That's true! Keeping the Ceremonial Law, or the Ten Commandments for that matter, will not save you. That's because the purpose of the Law is to *point out sin*, not to save us. Salvation comes by faith and faith alone in the saving grace of Jesus.

This brings us to **Colossians 2:16**: *"Let no man therefore judge you in meat, or in drink, or in respect of an holyday, or of the new moon or of the sabbath days."* This verse is probably used more than any other text in the entire Bible to try to prove that we no longer have to honor the Bible Sabbath. But is that what the verse is saying? If you have the misconception that the Ten Commandments were nailed to the cross you might get that idea. If you have viewed the Sabbath as ceremonial in nature, it may appear that way. But if you understand that it was the Ceremonial Law, with all its ordinances and sacrifices that ended with the death of Christ, then Colossians 2:16 begins to mean something completely different.

Let's back up a few verses and look at this text again beginning with verse 14: *"Blotting out the handwriting of **ordinance**s that was against us, which was contrary to us,* *and took it out of the way, nailing it to His cross."* (emphasis supplied). It's obvious from this text that something ended at the cross. But remember what we read earlier in Ephesians 2:15: *"Having abolished in His flesh the enmity, even the law of commandments contained in **ordinances...**"* (emphasis supplied). It was the Ceremonial Law, or the *"commandments contained in ordinances"* that ended with the death of Christ.

Look with me at Hebrews 8:13 and 9:1-3: *"In that he saith, A new covenant, he hath made the first old. Now that which decayeth and waxeth old is ready to vanish away. Then verily the first covenant had also **ordinances** of divine service, and a worldly sanctuary. For there was a tabernacle made; the first, wherein was the candlestick, and the table, and the shewbread; which is called the sanctuary. And after the second veil, the tabernacle which is called the Holiest of all."*

In Matthew 27:50,51 we are told that at the moment Christ died on the cross, the veil that separated the Holy Place from the Most Holy Place in the temple was torn in two from the top to the bottom, exposing the place where God's presence had been up to that time. This was done by an unseen hand to demonstrate that the sacrificial system was no longer needed. Why? Because the purpose of the sacrifice was to point the sinner forward to Christ, the Lamb of God (John 1:29). When Jesus died on the cross, the sacrificial system was nailed to the cross with Him.

Colossians 2:14-16 says: *"Blotting out the handwriting of ordinances that was against us, which was contrary to us, and took it out of the way, nailing it to His cross; And having spoiled principalities and powers, he made a show [KJV says shew]of them openly, triumphing over them in it. Let no man therefore judge you in meat, or in drink, or in respect of an holyday, or of the new moon, or of the sabbath days."*

Some people have erroneously concluded that Paul's statement here implies the abolition of the dietary restrictions given in Leviticus 11. But a careful study of Colossians 2 reveals that this was not Paul's intent. Under the Ceremonial Law, *meat offerings* and *drink offerings* were required to be offered along with the burnt offerings on the altar. Leviticus 23:13 says: *"And the meat offering thereof shall be two tenth deals of fine flour mingled with oil, an offering made by fire unto the Lord for a sweet savour: and the drink offering thereof shall be of wine, the fourth part of an hin."* You can read more about these meat and drink offerings in Numbers chapter 28. The apostle was not giving the Colossian Christians permission to eat unclean foods. What he is saying is that Christians are no longer obliged to carry out the meat and drink offering requirements of the Ceremonial Law.

You will also notice in Numbers 28:11 that the Israelites were commanded to have a special burnt offering at the beginning of each new month (this is the new moon referred to in Colossians 2:16). But what about the term *"sabbath days"* at the end of our text?

The word "Sabbath" comes from the Hebrew root *shbt* meaning "to cease from labor." God commanded all mankind to observe His weekly *ceasing* (or Sabbath) in the fourth commandment. Now remember that this weekly *ceasing* comes to us from God at creation, before the entrance of sin, and before the need of the Ceremonial Law. After sin, when the sacrificial system was instituted, and the Ceremonial Law was given on mount Sinai, God gave man other times of *ceasing* when He asked them not to labor as well. But these were yearly events (Passover, Pentecost, Day of Atonement, Feast of Trumpets, etc.), or *annual sabbaths*. (Those holy events were only called *sabbaths* because sabbath means "to cease from labor." God did not want Israel to work on those ritualistic holy days.) There is a sharp and fundamental distinction between the weekly Sabbath of the Moral Law, given before sin, and the annual ceremonial *sabbaths*, of the Ceremonial Law, that came about after sin. These typical *annual sabbaths* ended forever at the cross, when all types met their antitype in Jesus Christ.

Jamieson, Fausset, and Brown, in their *Commentary on the Whole Bible,* Zondervan, comments on Colossians 2:16, page 378, say: "The sabbaths of the day of atonement and feast of tabernacles have come to an end with the Jewish services to which they belonged. But the weekly Sabbath rests on a more permanent foundation, having been instituted in Paradise to commemorate the completion of creation in six days. Leviticus 23 expressly distinguishes 'the Sabbath of the Lord' from the other sabbaths."

The key to understanding the type of sabbath under consideration in Colossians 2:16 is found in verse 17: *"which are a shadow of things to come."* The weekly Sabbath is a memorial of an event at the beginning of earth's history. Hence, the "sabbath days" that Paul declares to be shadows pointing to Christ cannot refer to the weekly Sabbath of the fourth commandment, but must indicate the ceremonial rest days that reach their realization in Christ and His death as our sacrifice on Calvary's cross.

Albert Barnes, noted Presbyterian commentator, in his *Commentary on the New Testament,* says of Colossians 2:16: "There is not the slightest reason to believe that he [Paul] meant to teach that one of the Ten Commandments had ceased to be binding on mankind. If he had used the word in the singular number—'THE Sabbath'—it would then, of course, have been clear that he meant to teach that that commandment had ceased to be binding... But the use of the term in the plural number [sabbaths], show that he had his eye on the great number of days which were observed by the Hebrews as festivals... No part of the Moral Law—no one of the Ten Commandments—could be spoken of as 'a shadow of good things to come.'"

With this in mind, let us read Colossians 2:16 again: *"Let no man therefore judge you in meat* [meat offerings], *or in drink* [drink offerings], *or in respect of an holyday* [ceremonial feast days], *or of the new moon* [burnt offering at the beginning of each new month], *or of the sabbath days* [annual, ritualistic holy days such as Passover, Pentecost, Day of Atonement, etc., commanded under the Ceremonial Law]."

Paul is consistent by saying the same thing here in Colossians that he said in Galatians. He was telling the new converts to Christianity that they were no longer bound by the Ceremonial Law of Moses. Paul is saying here that the Ceremonial Law with its meat offerings, drink offerings, religious holydays, etc., foreshadowed, or pointed forward to Christ's sacrifice on the cross of Calvary.

THE SABBATH AND THE CEREMONIAL LAW

We have read repeated statements by Sundaykeeping Christians about the permanent, unchanging nature of the Ten Commandment Law. We have also read statements by these same Sundaykeeping Christians acknowledging the change of the Sabbath from the seventh to the first day of the week. By now we are all aware that the Sabbath is God's fourth commandment, and that the seventh day of the week is Saturday. This leaves us with an important question, just screaming for an answer. That question is, **"Would God have put the Sabbath in the middle of His Moral Law if the Sabbath were not a moral issue**?" You and I can say the Sabbath is not a moral issue all we want, but until God says it, it matters not! And then after we have faced that question, we all must ask ourselves, "How can a person acknowledge the Moral Law to be unchangeable, and still honor that change at the same time?" "How can a person know the Bible Sabbath to be Saturday, and still keep Sunday?"

The problem here is *not* one of insincerity. Rather, I believe it to be one of misconception. Most Sundaykeeping Christians today believe the fourth commandment to be ceremonial in nature. While they perceive nine of the commandments to be moral, they identify the fourth commandment with the Jewish Ceremonial Law. Now we just

81

read many statements that say that the Ceremonial Law ended at the cross. Does this mean that the seventh-day Sabbath ended at the cross as well? Is the Sabbath of the fourth commandment ceremonial in nature? Was it a "temporary" feature, for Old Testament times and the Jews only? I believe that we can answer these questions for ourselves if we follow some logic.

God instituted the Sabbath on the seventh day of the first week of time. It began at creation, *before* the entrance of sin. If man had never sinned, he would have continued keeping the Sabbath on the same seventh day that God, as Creator, "blessed" and "sanctified" at creation (Genesis 2:1-3). God gave man the Sabbath as a continual reminder and perpetual memorial, of a finished creation. That memorial *must remain* as long as creation remains. A memorial cannot be spiritualized away, and does not expire with the lapse of time. Inasmuch, then, as the Sabbath was instituted at creation, before the entrance of sin, it was an inseparable part of God's original plan and provision for man. It did not, therefore, have any ceremonial significance by forshadowing something to come. On the contrary, it was *memorial* in nature, not *ceremonial*.

The ceremonial system, on the other hand, was instituted *after* sin entered the world. There was no need for it prior to sin. It had the specific purpose of pointing the sinner forward to the coming Saviour. When Adam and Eve sinned, God took them to the east of Eden and made them *"coats of skins"* (Genesis 3:21). Where did He get those skins from? From the lambs of those first sacrifices when He explained to them the wages of sin (Genesis 4:4). The sacrificial system did not have its origin at mount Sinai as many Christians believe. It originated immediately after Adam and Eve sinned. It simply was not put into written form until Sinai. This ceremonial, sacrificial system would point man forward to *"The Lamb of God"* (John 1:29) who would one day become their ultimate sacrifice.

There was nothing ceremonial or typical about the act

of creation. The Sabbath command gives, as the very reason for its existence, that *"...in six days the Lord made heaven and earth, the sea, and all that in them is, and rested the seventh day: wherefore the Lord blessed the Sabbath day, and hallowed it."* (Exodus 20:11). The Sabbath of the Moral Law is anchored right back to the creation of this world. Philo called it "the birthday of the world." It is the celebration of the inauguration of human history. For the seventh-day Sabbath to be ceremonial, the time element would have had to be instituted *after* the entrance of sin, and the consequent need of a Saviour. Those who make the weekly Sabbath ceremonial reduce it from a creation ordinance to a Mosaic ordinance.

Let's look more specifically at the time element of the seventh day. Some Christians today believe that while the Sabbath principle is moral, eternal, and binding on us all, the specific time element is only ceremonial and temporary. This means they believe that while we must obey the fourth commandment, it's no longer important which day we obey it on. But when one thinks about the origin of the weekly cycle, one begins to realize that it really does matter which day we observe as the Sabbath.

Where does the weekly cycle come from? Does it come from the sun? No—the yearly cycle is governed by the sun. A year is the time it takes the earth to make a complete orbit around the sun. Does the weekly cycle come from the moon? No—the monthly cycle is governed by the moon. A month is the time it takes the moon to make a complete orbit around the earth. What about the earth turning on its axis? Does the weekly cycle come from this? No—the daily cycle is governed by this. A day is the time it takes the earth to make one complete rotation on its axis. The week is not based on any known astronomical measurement of time. *The Nautical Almanac*, 1931, page 740, says: "The period of seven days was reckoned independently of the month and in fact of all astronomical periods. From the Jewish Church it passed into the Christian Church." So where does the weekly cycle come from? It comes from *only one place*, and it has *only one purpose*. God set the seven day cycle in motion when He created this world. That is the one and only reason for its existence. God set the seventh-day Sabbath in motion at creation and brought it unflawed down to our day as a memorial (or an enshrining if you please) of that creation.

Clifford Goldstein wrote: "In every religion, men revere something—shrines, cities, even people. They kiss holy land; their ears clutch the syllables of holy men; they immerse themselves in holy water. Tangibles, touchables, holy things that they can see, revere, feel.

"In Genesis, however, the first thing declared holy is not a hill, a shrine, or a place, but a block of time, the seventh day. *'Then God blessed the seventh day and sanctified it'* (Genesis 2:3). The word *sanctified* is translated from the Hebrew *qadash*, which means 'to set apart for holy use.' Though Creation dealt with the heavens, the earth, the birds, the sea, and the beasts of the earth, all things of space—it was time, not space, that God first pronounced blessed and holy. This action makes sense, because, besides space, time is the dimension in which God's creation—the heavens, the earth, the birds, the sea, and the beasts of the earth—exist.

"Also, if God had made one specific place holy, a hill, a spring, a city, not all people would have easy access to it. They would have to travel to worship there. But time comes to us, instead of us going to it. Once a week...the Sabbath circles the globe. Arriving on one sundown, and leaving on the next, the seventh day washes over the planet each week like a huge cleansing wave. We never have to seek it. The day always finds us."

Goldstein continues: "Meanwhile, holy cities can be burned. Holy people can be killed. Holy shrines can be looted. But time is beyond the fire and knife. No man can touch, much less destroy it. Therefore, by making a special time holy, God has made the Sabbath invincible... We can no more stop the Sabbath than we can the sunrise. God protected His memorial to the objects of space, which are vulnerable to men, by placing it in time, which is not.

"Finally, men can avoid holy things. They can hide from objects, people, places. But they can't flee from time. We can ignore it, be ignorant of it, hate it, but the Sabbath always comes, and nothing, no one, can stop it." *A Pause for Peace*, 1992, pages 46,47.

Any theologian will tell you that the number seven has great significance in Scripture. It was used to express *totality*, *completion* and *perfection*. Peter, for instance, expected Jesus' approval for proposing to extend forgiveness to his brother up to this perfect limit of seven. Jesus replied by admonishing Peter to multiply that seven by "seventy times." The Israelites marched seven days around Jericho, following seven priests, blowing seven trumpets. And then on the seventh day they marched around Jericho another seven times before the walls fell down. Revelation speaks of seven churches, seven seals, seven trumpets, seven thunders, seven plagues, and seven candlesticks. The special significance of seven in Scripture cannot be ignored. But how did the number seven come to acquire this meaning of completion and perfection? It is *without a doubt* the result of its association with the weekly cycle and the seventh day of creation. The seventh-day Sabbath is God's symbol of completion and perfection. And the Sabbath's weekly recurrence is designed to remind us of our roots, and to heighten our awareness that our Creator still sustains us each and every day of our lives.

Understanding now that the seven day cycle has no function whatsoever outside of directing our hearts and minds back to our Creator God—and knowing that God has preserved that seven day cycle, unflawed, down to our day—and understanding that He has enshrined the Sabbath as a memorial of His great act of creating—could you look your Creator in the face and tell Him that the significance *He* has attached to that holy memorial doesn't matter to you? Could you look Him in the face and tell Him it doesn't matter on which day you honor that memorial? Could you face Him in the judgment and tell Him that *His*

Sabbath has no significance to you? Be sure of one thing, dear reader, you will face your Creator in the judgment.

A QUESTION OF DAYS

Many Christians believe that Romans 14:5 gives them the right to keep any day they choose to keep. But is that really what Paul is saying? Romans 14:5 says: *"One man esteemeth one day above another: another esteemeth every day alike. Let every man be fully persuaded in his own mind."* The emphasis of Romans 14 is not about which day is proper to keep, but rather it is a discussion of not judging, or condemning another person. Paul is saying that no man should coerce another to believe as he does; that the observer or nonobserver is answerable only to God. He is saying that if a man keeps a certain day, he must do it only if he is *"fully persuaded in his own mind."* Whether Paul is referring to the Sabbath of the Moral Law, or to the ritualistic days of the Ceremonial Law in verse 5, is unclear by reading the text. But the principle of not judging another would hold true no matter what the content of the passage.

In trying to understand Paul's intent in Romans 14:5, one must consider the content of the rest of the book. In Romans 2:12 Paul says that men will be judged by the law; in 3:20 that it is by the law that we have the knowledge of sin; in 3:31 that faith establishes the law in our hearts; in 6:1,2 that grace saves from its transgression; in 8:4 that the demands of the law are met by those in Christ; and in 8:7 that the carnal mind is at enmity with the law. Those to whom Paul wrote this epistle were commandment keepers, therefore Romans 14:5 cannot be made to mean that Paul spoke against the Sabbath of the Ten Commandments.

Another text that speaks of the observance of days is found in Galatians 4:10,11. It reads: *"Ye observe days, and months, and times, and years. I am afraid of you, lest I have bestowed upon you labour in vain."* If you have ever used these verses to try to prove that we do not have to keep the fourth commandment, or at least that we do not have to keep it on the seventh day of the week, you are completely wrong in your interpretation. In verse 8 Paul says: *"Howbeit then, when ye **knew not God,** ye did service unto them which by nature are no gods."* (emphasis supplied). Before they knew God, before the gospel came to them, they were heathen. The oldest and most widespread heathen worship was sun worship, and the oldest heathen holy day was "the day of the sun." When the Galatians backslid from Christianity, they doubtless returned to their old heathen feasts and festivals and holydays. In Galatians 4 the apostle Paul is questioning their conversion to Jesus Christ, and laying before them the *"beggarly elements"* (verse 9) of heathenism to which they were in *"bondage"* before he had preached Jesus to them.

DID JESUS ENUMERATE
NINE COMMANDMENTS?

Many of my Sundaykeeping Christian friends believe that Jesus abolished the Ten Commandments at the cross, and then enumerated nine of them again in the New Testament, leaving out the Sabbath command. If you have heard this, or if you have taught this, you are not alone. But you need to know that Jesus nowhere enumerated the Ten Commandments. He quoted *some of them* in Matthew 19 to show the Rich Young Ruler that he was not really keeping them, but His intent was never to reinstate some while leaving others out.

Those who teach that Christ reinstated nine of the commandments in the New Testament need to consider that nowhere in the teachings of Jesus is there any reference ever made to the second commandment. One also needs to consider Jesus' prophecy of the Sabbath in Matthew 24. Jesus ascended back to heaven in A.D. 31. In Matthew 24 He prophesied the destruction of Jerusalem that took place in A.D. 70. He was not preaching to Jews here, but to His Christian disciples *"privately"* (verse 3), when He told them in verse 20 to pray that they would not have to flee Jerusalem *"in the winter, neither on the Sabbath day."* For forty years they prayed at His request that their flight from Jerusalem might not fall on the Sabbath day. The fourth commandment was clearly intended to still be in force after Christ's ascension.

Ask yourself the question, "Why should we demand that Jesus restate the Ten Commandments in the New Testament?" The answer to that question lies only in the fact that many Christians lump both the Moral and the Ceremonial laws into one, and abolish all law at the cross. Because some link the Sabbath command with Judaism and ceremonialism, they try to make a case for its nonexistence in the New Testament. I believe that Matthew 24:20 should dispel any such belief.

TWO NEW COMMANDMENTS

Many people ask, **Aren't the two new commandments proof that Jesus did away with the Ten Commandment Law**? The answer again is "no". Let's look at those two new commandments in Matthew chapter 22.

Matthew 22:23-28 tells us that the Sadducees (they didn't believe in the resurrection) were trying to trap Jesus with a trick question about the resurrection. Verses 29-33 tell us that Jesus made them look rather foolish when He answered their trick question without being trapped. Verses 34 and 35 say: *"But when the Pharisees had heard that He had put the Sadducees to silence, they were gathered together. Then one of them, which was a lawyer, asked Him a question, tempting Him..."*

Because the Sadducees were not able to trap Jesus, the Pharisees thought they would try their hand at it. They found someone who was very articulate, a lawyer, and he asked Jesus a question that ordinarily would have been impossible to answer without being trapped. They asked Him in verse 36: *"Master, which is the great command-*

ment in the law?" They were trying to trap Jesus into saying one of the Ten Commandments first. Had Jesus said any one of the commandments, no matter which one He would have started with (because they are all equal), the lawyer would have screamed, "Aha! He puts more weight on this one commandment than on all the rest!" You can see how desperate they were to trap Jesus. They wanted to kill Him, and they would stoop to any depth to do it.

Do you remember the story about the young man who tried to trick the wise old man by asking him, "Is the little bird in my hand dead or alive?" There was no way the wise old man could answer that question correctly. Had he said "alive," the young man would have broken its neck with his finger and shown him a dead bird. Had he said "dead," the young man would have opened his hand and let the little bird fly away. It was a trick question. So the wise old man simply answered, "That depends on you, my son."

This is exactly what Jesus did in Matthew 22. Rather than fall into their trap, He answered them perfectly in verses 37-39: *"Jesus said unto him* [the lawyer], *Thou shalt love the Lord thy God with all thy heart, and with all thy soul, and with all thy mind. This is the first and great commandment. And the second is like unto it, Thou shalt love thy neighbor as thyself."* Jesus answered the lawyer's question with just as much skill as He had answered the question asked by the Sadducees.

What does Jesus' answer have to do with the Ten Commandments? The first four commandments are all directed toward *love to God.* The last six commandments express *love to man.* After carefully avoiding their trap, Jesus finished His comments to them in verse 40 by saying: *"On these two commandments hang all the law and the prophets."*

Instead of *replacing* the Ten Commandments, the two new commandments are simply a *summary* of the ten. Paul told us exactly the same thing in Romans 13:9: *"For this, Thou shalt not commit adultery, Thou shalt not kill, Thou shalt not steal, Thou shalt not bear false witness, Thou shalt not covet; and if there be any other commandment, it is briefly comprehended in this saying, namely, Thou shalt love thy neighbor as thyself."*

Baptist pastor William M. Fletcher wrote: "Jesus summarized the keeping of the Ten Commandments in terms of love. He spoke of Godward love first, then of manward love. These statements, he said, summarize all of the Ten Commandments and all that the prophets taught. The first command deals with our walk with God, the second with our behavior among men. It is no accident that his answer is given in this order: first, God did give the commandments in this order [see Exodus 20]. Second, this is the order in which we must obey them. When the vertical relationship is right, our relationships on the horizontal plane are apt to be right. When our experience of God's love is daily, soul-inspiring and life-changing, then our capacity to love others will also be growing. Then we'll begin to find we are compelled to reach out." William M. Fletcher, *The Second Greatest Commandment,* 1983, pages 30,31.

The famous preacher Spurgeon wrote: "Does any man say to me, 'You see, then, instead of the ten commandments we have received the two commandments, and these are much easier.' I answer that this reading of the law is not in the least easier. Such a remark implies a want of thought and experience. Those two precepts comprehend the ten at their fullest extent, and cannot be regarded as the erasure of a jot or tittle of them." Charles H. Spurgeon, "The Perpetuity Of The Law Of God," *Spurgeon's Expository Encyclopedia,* by Baker.

THE SABBATH AND THE CROSS

Genesis chapter one takes us step by step through the first six days of creation week. Verse 31 says: *"And God saw every thing that He had made, and, behold, it was very good. And the evening and the morning were the sixth day."* Luke calls that sixth day the "preparation" (Luke

23:54), meaning it is a day to prepare oneself for the Sabbath. And on that sixth day of creation, the day we now call Friday, God formulated His masterpiece. He created a pair of living, breathing human beings. Verse 27 says: *"So God created man in His own image, in the image of God created He him; male and female created He them."*

In Mark 2:27 Jesus said, *"The Sabbath was made for man..."* God knew that man would need a weekly reservation of uninterrupted time to remain close to his Maker. So at the end of that first Friday of creation week, with Adam and Eve at His side, God made the Sabbath. Beginning with Genesis 2:2 we read: *"And on the seventh day God ended His work which He had made; and He rested on the seventh day from all His work which He had made. And God blessed the seventh day, and sanctified it: because that in it He had rested from all His work which God created and made."* Just think, if Adam and Eve needed Sabbath rest in paradise, how much more do you and I need it today!

God finished creation in six days, and then invited His children to share in the celebration of *His* work. Adam and Eve rested with God, and by doing so, acknowledged the work that *He* had done in their behalf. After all, this is the purpose of the Sabbath. It points us away from ourselves and our own works, so that we can value the work that God has done for us.

George Vandeman wrote: "This Sabbath rest in God's finished work symbolizes what Christianity stands for. Other world religions focus upon human "realization"— what we can do to help ourselves. But Christians celebrate God's accomplishments on our behalf. That's why the Sabbath points us away from ourselves, away from our works, so we can value what God has done." George E. Vandeman, *When God Made Rest*, 1987, page 19.

Justin Edward said, "Had all men properly kept the Sabbath all would have known Jehovah, and worshipped from the creation of the world to the present time, and idolatry would never have been practiced on the earth."

91

But unfortunately that is not what happened. You know the sad story all too well. Adam and Eve disobeyed and changed God's plan for their happiness. God told them if they sinned they would have to die, and on the day they strayed from Him, that death process began. Genesis chapter 3 tells us that God took Adam and Eve out of Eden and made them *"coats of skins"* (verse 21). Where did He get those skins from? What must one do in order to have clothing made from skins?

On that dark day outside of Eden God took the life of that first innocent lamb. He did this to show Adam and Eve that death is the consequence for sin. Revelation 13:8 tells us that Christ is *"the Lamb slain from the foundation of the world."* God explained to our first parents the wages of sin, and then told them that the lamb would represent the Saviour, or the substitute who would someday die in their place. Yes, the plan of salvation had its origin way back at the east of Eden, and every bleeding lamb of the Old Testament reminded the repenting sinner that one day a Substitute would die in their place.

Now that we have allowed our imaginations to scan creation and the fall, move ahead with me about four thousand years to a hill outside of Jerusalem. It's another Friday afternoon. Amid the shameful laughter and jeers of the crowd, Jesus hangs dying on a wooden cross. The same Creator who formed our first parents now hangs in open shame as the substitute for a lost race. And as the afternoon sun begins to fade, He cries, "It is finished!" and closes His eyes in death. His friends lovingly remove His lifeless body from the cross and lay Him in the tomb where He remains over the hours of the Sabbath (Luke 23:56). He who rested at the end of creation, now rests at the end of redemption.

"We can see why Jesus proclaimed Himself 'Lord of the Sabbath.' Because the Sabbath commemorates His two greatest acts on our behalf—creating us and saving us. These are the reasons we worship Him. And we express our faith in Christ as our Maker and Redeemer by sharing

His Sabbath rest. Every Friday evening as the sun goes down, millions of Christians around the world stop working. They set aside their unfinished business to celebrate the finished work of Jesus." Ibid, pages 20,21.

The next time someone tries to tell you that Sabbathkeeping is an attempt to gain salvation by works, tell them that nothing could be further from the truth. The word "Sabbath" comes from the Hebrew meaning "to cease, desist, rest"—the exact opposite of works. The Sabbath points us away from our own works and invites us to rest in Christ's work for us.

GOD'S REASON IS ENOUGH

A friend of mine said recently, "I see no reason for keeping a day holy." And my answer to him was, "We don't have to see the reasoning. If God said it, that is all the reason we need."

What if Peter had taken the same attitude as my friend? Jesus told him to go catch a fish and he would find the needed tax money in the fish's mouth (Matthew 17). Peter could have responded, "I see no reason for looking for money in a fish's mouth. That's not where money is found. If you want money you go to a bank!" What a blessing Peter would have missed had he not obeyed. What God asks us to do does not have to make sense to us.

Naaman was told to dip in the Jordan River seven times and he would be healed (2 Kings 5). His first response was one of anger. He could not see the reasoning behind bathing in a muddy river to heal leprosy. Had he not reconsidered and obeyed without question, he would never have been cured.

Wordsworth wrote: "In doing only things of which we ourselves see the reason, we may be only obeying ourselves and not obeying God. Therefore Almighty God tests our faith by things of which we do not see the reason." Bishop Wordsworth, *Commentary on the Holy Bible,* Volume 1, page 272.

DOES IT REALLY MATTER?

We have more than ample evidence today as to which day the seventh-day Sabbath is. It is the fourth commandment and it is just as important to God as any of the other commandments are. Yet I am constantly asked the question, **But does it really matter? Does it really matter which day I keep? As long as I keep one day in seven, isn't that all right with God?**

One day as I was working in my study, the door bell rang. I opened the door and was warmly greeted by a nice elderly couple. The smiles on their faces and the Bibles under their arms told me they were very excited about their church, and they invited me to attend the following Sunday. I told them I would be delighted to visit their church, and then invited them to visit mine. They said it would be impossible for them to visit my church because they had duties every Sunday in their own church and couldn't get away. I told them that I went to church on Saturday so it shouldn't interfere with their Sunday responsibilities.

"Saturday!" they exclaimed, and the happy look disappeared. "Don't you know that Jesus did away with the Sabbath?" he asked.

"No, I don't know that," I said. "Is that in the Bible?"

"Why yes!" he said, "We only have to keep nine of the commandments now. The Bible says that if we break one of the nine commandments that we are guilty of breaking them all."

I asked the gentleman if the Bible says "nine?"

"Yes it says nine," he said. "I attended a popular Bible College and learned that it says nine."

"Please show me where the Bible says that we only have to keep nine of the commandments," I asked.

He began to leaf through his Bible looking for the text. As he was looking he kept repeating these words, "If you break one of the nine commandments, you are guilty of breaking them all."

After what seemed to be ten minutes I said, "I believe you are looking for James 2:10." He quickly turned to it and this is what it says: *"For whosoever shall keep the whole law, and yet offend in one point, he is guilty of all."*

I was doing my best to love that dear couple without embarrassing them, but I felt that they needed to know that they were misquoting Scripture. He then tried to cover up his embarrassment by asking the question, "Does it really matter anyway?"

Whenever I hear someone ask, "Does it really matter which day I keep?", I feel that what they are really asking is, "How particular is God?"

HOW PARTICULAR IS GOD?

Turn with me to Exodus 4:24 and let's read: *"And it came to pass by the way in the inn, that the Lord met him, and sought to kill him."* Whom did the Lord meet, and why did He seek to kill him?

It seems rather strange to us that God would try to kill someone in a hotel room, but this is exactly what happened to Moses. Why did God seek to kill him? Because God gave Moses an explicit command and Moses did not do it. Verses 25 and 26 tell us that Moses' wife Zipporah performed the circumcision that God commanded Moses to perform, and only then did the Lord let Moses go. When God asks us to do something, does it really matter to Him if we do it or not? Of course it does.

Look at the story of Cain and Abel. God told them to offer a burnt offering upon the altar. They were to offer a lamb of the first year without blemish. This lamb was to represent Christ and to show them that their sins would cause His death some day. Abel did exactly as God asked, but Cain thought he knew better. He brought a substitute from his garden as an offering instead. You can read all about it there in Genesis chapter 4. God rejected Cain's offering because he did not do exactly as God commanded. God is a merciful God, but he is also a particular God.

What about Adam and Eve? God told them that they could eat of every tree in the garden except the tree of the knowledge of good and evil (Genesis 2:15-17). Why a tree? Adam and Eve could have reasoned that all the trees look the same. They could have said, "As long as we don't eat of one of the trees (and we'll choose which one) God should be happy."

That's the way many Christians reason today about the day they keep as the Sabbath. They say, "As long as we keep one day in seven God should be happy." But God said to Adam and Eve that it had to be *that* tree. God said, "I'll choose the tree, and you must obey." You see, the tree was a test of obedience. Friends, God is a loving God, but He is also a particular God. And He is a consistent God. He could have made the test any number of things, but *He* chose a tree. The issue with the tree was obedience. The issue with the day is obedience as well. Dr. Jack Provonsha, in his book, *God Is With Us*, has asked us to imagine the consequences had God blessed and sanctified a stone as the sign of His creative power instead of a day. All roads would have converged to the place where this stone lay. Man would have built a shrine around it and adorned it with every kind of honor imaginable. And Dr. Provonsha suggests that eventually man would have worshipped the stone rather than God.

Ezekiel 20:20 says: *"And hallow* [keep holy] *my Sabbaths; and they shall be a **sign** between me and you, that ye may know that I am the Lord your God."* (emphasis supplied). The Sabbath (as well as the other commandments) can be considered a test of obedience to us. Are we going to reason that it doesn't matter which day we keep?

You might be tempted to think, "Oh, but that's all Old Testament. God isn't so particular in the New Testament." Isn't He? Turn with me to Acts 5 and read about Ananias and Sapphira. It's recorded there in verses 1-11 for all to see. Ananias and his wife Sapphira had promised God that when they sold a piece of property they were going to give all the money to the church. It so happened that when the property sold they kept back part of the money. Now God didn't tell them that they had to give all the money to the church. They offered the money freely themselves. But then when they did not give it all as they had pledged, they were being dishonest with God. Verses 5 and 10 tell us that they fell dead at Peter's feet. God is a loving God, but He is also a particular God. How can we reason today that He is not particular about one of His Ten Commandments?

Malachi 3:6 says: *"For I am the Lord, I change not..."* If the Lord was particular back then, He is just as particular today. Hebrews 13:8 says: *"Jesus Christ the same yesterday, and to day, and for ever."*

Does my salvation depend on my keeping the Sabbath? Let me say that I believe that there will be many people in heaven who never knew about the seventh-day Sabbath. They lived up to the Word of God to the best of their ability, but died without ever hearing about the Sabbath. But for those of us who know what God expects of us and do not do it, that's a different story. Yes, I believe that our eternal salvation depends on our desire to follow God's will when we become aware of it.

The Ten Commandments are still binding on us all. In fact the Bible tells us that the Ten Commandments will be the standard for the judgment at the end of the world. Ecclesiastes 12:13,14 says: *"Let us hear the conclusion of the whole matter: Fear God, and keep His commandments: for this is the whole duty of man. For God shall bring every work into judgment, with every secret thing, whether it be good, or whether it be evil."* We find the same thought carried through into the New Testament in James 2:10-12: *"For whosoever shall keep the whole law, and yet offend in one point, he is guilty of all. For He that said, Do not commit adultery, said also, Do not kill. Now if thou commit no adultery, yet if thou kill, thou art become a transgressor of the law. So speak ye, and so do, as they that shall be judged by the law of liberty."* Dwight L. Moody wrote: "These Ten Commandments are not ten different laws; they are one law. If I am held up in the air by a chain

97

with ten links, and I break one of them, down I come, just as surely as if I break the whole ten. Dwight L. Moody, *Weighed and Wanting*, pages 119-124. Whether a person lived in Old Testament times or New, he will be judged by the same standard—the Ten Commandments.

God expects us to endeavor to live up to all the light that we have. John 12:35 says: *"Then Jesus said unto them, Yet a little while is the light with you. Walk while ye have the light, lest darkness come upon you: for he that walketh in darkness knoweth not whither he goeth."* I remember, as a young boy growing up on a farm in Colorado, that I was afraid of the dark. I had my older brother to thank for that. I remember having to go out and shut the chicken house door many times after dark because I had neglected to do so earlier. My heart would pound all the way out there, and I would run all the way back. One night I dropped the flashlight as I was running back to the house. There was no way that I was going to go back and get it; I just kept on running. I can remember stumbling over all kinds of things. That is what I think about when I read this verse: *"Walk while ye have the light, lest darkness come upon you: for he that walketh in darkness knoweth not whither he goeth."*

Another text that expresses this same thought is found in 1 John 1:6,7. It says: *"If we say that we have fellowship with Him, and walk in darkness, we lie, and do not the truth: But if we walk in the light, as He is in the light, we have fellowship one with another, and the blood of Jesus Christ His Son cleanseth us from all sin."*

Does this sound a bit like legalism to you? It shouldn't. It's merely what the Bible says. Obedience to the Law of God is not the way to salvation initially. Obedience is meaningless without a relationship with Jesus. And yet, after one is saved, he cannot retain that relationship with Jesus without obedience. Jesus said in John 14:15: *"If you love me, keep my commandments."* We are not to keep the commandments *in order to* be saved. We are to keep them *because we are* saved. Obedience is a *love response.*

Because I love Jesus, I want to do what He has asked me to do. I want to do everything I can to please Him. In John 15:14 Jesus said: *"Ye are my friends, if ye do whatsoever I command you."* Obedience is proof of our friendship with Him. Remember the old saying, "The proof of the pudding is in the eating?" The proof of the relationship is in the obedience. 1 John 2:3 says: *"And hereby we do know that we know Him, if we keep His commandments."* Some people view obedience as optional, but there is nothing optional about it. The Ten Commandments are not multiple choice!

Many Christians today believe that to observe the Sabbath on the seventh day of the week involves the observer automatically in legalism. But the question must be addressed: in precisely what way, and on what Scriptural authority, can regard for the Sabbath involve a person automatically in legalism? Was God legalistic because He rested on the seventh day of creation week? Is God legalistic because He commands us to keep holy the seventh day of the week? Is it more legalistic to worship on the seventh day than it is to worship on the first day of the week? Would it be more legalistic to worship on Saturday than on Wednesday? And if it was *not* legalistic for God to rest on the seventh day, why should it be legalistic for us to follow His example and *"walk, even as He walked."* (1 John 2:6). What logic is there in the thought that it is legalistic for us to observe the seventh day, but not for God to do so?

No Sundaykeeping Christian would call the sixth commandment, *"Thou shalt not kill,"* legalistic. In fact, many openly protest and march against abortion. And this is their right. It is *not* legalistic to take this commandment literally. And Jesus was not legalistic when He enlarged on this commandment by saying that even if a person is angry with his brother he is guilty of murder already in his heart (Matthew 5:21,22).

No Sundaykeeping Christian would call the seventh commandment, *"Thou shalt not commit adultery,"* legalistic. And Jesus was not legalistic when He enlarged on it by saying that anyone who lusts after another is guilty already in his heart (Matthew 5:27,28).

Dear reader, I protest against the reasoning prevalent in Christianity today that makes it legalistic to observe the seventh day of the week, but not legalistic to observe the first day of the week. Such reasoning is inconsistent with sound logic.

Robert Shuler writes: "The keeping of the seventh day by a renewed soul is not legalism, nor is it contrary to salvation by grace, In fact, the Sabbath commandment is the only precept in the law that stands as a sign of deliverance from sin and sanctification by grace alone." Robert Shuler, *God's Everlasting Sign*, page 90.

The Jewish nation had distorted the Sabbath and turned it into a burden. They devised their own list of rules to make sure that no one broke the Sabbath by mistake. The Pharisees had come to believe that God loved people to the extent to which they kept these rules and regulations. But God never intended the Sabbath to be burdened down like this. The Pharisees forbade people to squeeze the juice out of a piece of fruit on the Sabbath, or to eat an egg that had been laid on the Sabbath. They forbade people to walk two miles, to sew two stitches, to lift two dried figs, to write two numbers, or even to erase two numbers on the Sabbath. In their zeal they bogged the whole Jewish nation down in an endless parade of details. By the time of Christ, the Sabbath had become so burdened with man-made rules that the Jews lost sight of both the Sabbath and the Lord of the Sabbath. Jesus came on a mission of restoration. He came to show that *"the Sabbath was made for man, and not man for the Sabbath."* (Mark 2:27). He came to show us what proper Sabbath observance should be.

Because Jesus did not do things the way the Jews thought He should, they were constantly accusing Him of Sabbath breaking. They had a terrible hatred for Jesus, and this hatred eventually led them to take His life. There are many today who have this same spirit of enmity toward true Sabbathkeeping. They call those who try to follow God by keeping the Sabbath a "cult." They say all manner of evil against these Christians and accuse them of being deceived. Jesus said in Matthew 5:19: *"Whosoever therefore shall break one of these least commandments, and shall teach men so, he shall be called least in the kingdom of heaven* [meaning that he will be the least worthy of the kingdom of heaven]: *but whosoever shall do and teach them, the same shall be called great in the kingdom of heaven."* Jesus in no way implied that one who breaks the commandments will be in heaven. On the contrary, He always taught that the kingdom of heaven is for those who love Him and are obedient to Him. Albert Barnes, commenting on Matthew 5:19, said: "Anyone who considers any command of God so unimportant as not to be obeyed is unworthy of His kingdom."

Someday there will come a *"restitution of all things"* (Acts 3:21). Then the creation Sabbath; the Sabbath that Christ made (for He was our Creator, John 1:3; Colossians 1:16,17; Hebrews 1:1,2); the Sabbath that Christ kept; the Sabbath that Christ asked us to keep, will still be a day of rest and worship of God. Isaiah 66:22,23 says: *"For as the new heavens and the new earth, which I will make, shall remain before me, saith the Lord, so shall your seed and your name remain. And it shall come to pass, that from one new moon to another, and from one Sabbath to another, shall all flesh come to worship before me, saith the Lord."* The Sabbath of Eden lost will still be observed in Eden restored.

A PASTOR'S TESTIMONY

Raymond Holmes pastored a Sundaykeeping church for many years before he really came to grips with the issue of the Bible Sabbath. Today he keeps the seventh-day Sabbath and teaches at a seminary in Michigan. What follows are excerpts from his book, *Stranger In My Home:*

"When one faces the issue squarely and does not permit ages of church tradition and contemporary culture to determine the conclusion, the clarity of the seventh-day Sabbath is startling. The Decalogue, the Ten Commandments, commands the observance of the seventh-day Sabbath. However, it did not originate there. The seventh-day Sabbath was part of creation. God set it apart for all of mankind. Therefore the argument that of all the commandments the Sabbath commandment pertains only to the Jews, does not stand up. Nowhere does the Biblical account make such a distinction, whereas tradition and/or culture does.

"If we apply the Protestant principle of Bible interpretation which holds that the Bible is to be interpreted literally unless the context indicates otherwise, then more than the principle of Sabbath observance is valid. The specific day itself is also part of faithfulness to the commandment. Furthermore, the observance of the seventh-day Sabbath was not simply a part of Jewish culture anymore than the other nine. Individuals have challenged Sabbath observance by saying there is no difference between one day and the next. My answer is: 'That is true, except if God has spoken and declared there is a difference.' If God has spoken then that ought to be enough.

"Our Lord's criticism of tradition as religious criteria appears in Matthew 15:1-9 and Mark 7:5-13. He accuses the Scribes and Pharisees of transgressing God's commandment in favor of their own tradition and, by so doing, nullifying the Word of God. Jesus quoted Isaiah 29:13 to them: *This people honors me with their lips, but their heart is far from me; in vain do they worship me, teaching as doctrines the precepts of men.'* (Matthew 15:8,9). Christ's words made it clear that I could not, and must not, follow tradition but the Word of God."

Holmes continues: "The hallowing of the seventh-day Sabbath immediately followed the creation of humans. God created people dependent upon Him and with the need to rest and worship. Next He provided them with the time and opportunity to do so. Furthermore, He motivated us to rest and worship by attaching the blessing of holiness to the seventh day. The Sabbath was to be the memorial of creation by which God would be perpetually acknowledged as Creator and the source of life. It would also assist people in acknowledging their dependence upon God.

"Therefore, we cannot consider it legalistic to observe the seventh-day Sabbath. Rather, it is an act of faith in response to a loving Creator and Redeemer. However, we can rightly regard it as legalistic to observe a day which God did not command and hallow and which only human tradition has established. Biblical, historical, and theological evidence all indicate that God created the seventh-day Sabbath for the benefit of all people, and that He has never abrogated it...

"The Gospels clearly indicate Christ's attitude toward the Sabbath. Consider Luke 4:16: *'And He came to Nazareth, where He had been brought up; and He went to the synagogue, as His custom was, on the Sabbath day.'* Proponents of Sunday observance, and I was one of them, explain away such passages on the grounds that His evangelistic zeal took Him to the place where, and at times when, He knew people would gather. But notice the emphasis in the verse upon His *'custom.'* In other words, He habitually went to the Synagogue on the Sabbath because He was obedient to His Father's will. His custom involved not only His evangelistic concern, but also His own personal piety and observance of the day.

"Jesus took the Sabbath out of the legalistic context Jewish tradition had evolved about it and put it into the context of grace when He said: *'The Son of man is Lord even of the Sabbath.'* He didn't say the Sabbath no longer existed. Nor did He say that He Himself would take the place of the Sabbath in the same way that He became the Paschal Lamb. He did, however, declare that he is the Sabbath's Lord. In other words, Sabbath observance must begin with faith in Him! Therefore, no person can rightly keep the seventh day as the Biblical Sabbath until or unless

103

he acknowledges Jesus Christ as Lord. Sabbath rest begins with rest from sin by faith in the Sin Bearer and Saviour. True Sabbathkeeping is not legalistic works, but represents a faith/love response to the person of Jesus Christ..." C. Raymond Holmes, *Stranger In My Home*, Pointer Publications, 1987, pages 74-77.

I REST MY CASE

Acts 17:22 says that Paul stood on Mars' Hill in Athens and pleaded his case for Christianity. Scripture tells us that some who heard him believed, and others did not. That seems always to be the scenario.

I too have pleaded my case. The evidence before us is *overwhelming*. The arguments against are few and weak. Some who read will listen and believe. Others will wish to throw stones as many did at Paul. But the issues before us are far too important for a mere casual glance. I entreat you to prayfully ask the Holy Spirit to guide you as you restudy verse by verse the material before you. What do you have to lose?

Do you love Jesus as I love Him? He gave His life for you; are you willing to give your life for Him? If today He asked you not to eat of the fruit of a certain tree would you obey Him—or would you stubbornly persist in questioning His judgment in order to have your own way? If He asked you to honor Him by keeping a certain day as "holy time," would you obey Him? He hung between two rusty nails for you and me, friend. He did so much for us that our answer should be a resounding "YES!, I will obey Him."

There are thousands of people each day, in every country of this world, who make the decision to follow Jesus all the way in rejecting the human tradition of Sunday keeping. Won't you join them and gladly follow the divine command: *"Remember the Sabbath day to keep it holy?"*

104

Love Makes Obedience

Love makes obedience a thing of joy!
To do the will of one we like to please
Is never hardship, though it tax our strength;
Each privilege of service love will seize!

Love makes us loyal, glad to do or go,
And eager to defend a name or cause;
Love takes the drudgery from common work,
And asks no rich reward or great applause.

Love gives us satisfaction in our task,
And wealth in learning lessons of the heart;
Love sheds a light of glory on our toil
And makes us humbly glad to have a part.

Love makes us choose to do the will of God,
To run His errands and proclaim His truth;
It gives our hearts an eager, lilting song;
Our feet are shod with tireless wings of youth!

Hazel Hartwell Simon